Cristyle Wood Egitto

WINNIPEG

JAN 2 1 2021

PUBLIC LIBRARY

111 Places
in Palm Beach
That You Must
Not Miss

Photographs by Jakob Takos

D1002784

emons:

To Emilia and Audrey.
I adore you.

© Emons Verlag GmbH
All rights reserved
Photographs by Jakob Takos, except see p. 238
Cover icon: shutterstock.com/Nopkamon Tanayakorn
Edited by Karen E. Seiger
Maps: altancicek.design, www.altancicek.de
Basic cartographical information from Openstreetmap,
OpenStreetMap-Mitwirkende, ODbL
Printing and binding: Grafisches Centrum Cuno, Calbe
Printed in Germany 2020
ISBN 978-3-7408-0897-6
First edition

Did you enjoy this guidebook? Would you like to see more?
Join us in uncovering new places around the world on:
www.111places.com

Foreword

One of the most devastating times of my life turned out to be one of the greatest blessings. In August 1992, Hurricane Andrew claimed my family's home in Homestead, FL. Taking shelter on Singer Island in my aunt and uncle's winter house, I began my time in Palm Beach.

I was raised in North County, where I eventually attended William T. Dwyer High School and met my future husband, Andrew. After graduating from UF (Go Gators!) I moved to Charlotte, NC, but I was always drawn back to the water. The beach, the boats, even waterfront dining is where I feel the most at peace. So when Andrew and I decided to have kids, we made the move back home. I started the food blog *EatPalmBeach* as a way to rediscover our hometown after years away and fell in love with it all over again.

While people know Palm Beach for our glitzy resorts, lush golf courses, and pristine beaches, we are a beautifully diverse area with layers to uncover. Our history is rich, sometimes dark, and truly fascinating. We have been the playground of socialites, the second home of billionaires, and a vital hub along the development of the Southeast. But we are also the place to go for unique American pioneer stories, unexpected curiosities, and unimaginable natural beauty.

I invite Palm Beach locals and visitors to dive into this book because there is so much to learn and appreciate about this wonderful place. Take in the masterpieces of Norton Museum of Art, and enjoy a coffee at Pumphouse Coffee Roasters. Witness a turtle hatching with Loggerhead Marinelife Center, explore the parks overlooking the iconic Jupiter Lighthouse, and take flight at Shark Wake Park 561. It's time to experience Palm Beach through a new lens – even our "tourist traps" have much deeper histories.

It has been my honor to write this book. I have loved exploring, compiling, and telling our story (and some of our secrets) through these 111 locations. It's an absolute dream come true.

111 Places

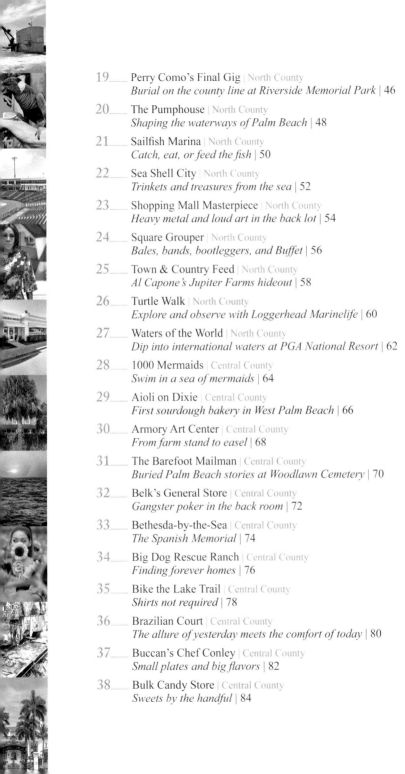

1 9/11 Memorial Plaza

Steel at Fire Station 3

Nestled around a monument of steel obtained from the World Trade Center in New York City, 9/11 Memorial Plaza rests in front of Fire Station 3, a symbol of the fallen towers and nearly 3,000 lives lost on September 11, 2001. The Fire Rescue Department of Palm Beach Gardens procured and commissioned the sculpture as a non-profit, public artwork. The centerpiece steel fragment, tagged C-89, was from the lower levels (floors 12-15) of the South Tower and stands approximately three stories tall.

Mark Fuller was the artist behind the memorial, which features eight-foot glass panels with the names of people who lost their lives that day in an arrangement mimicking the Maltese cross, a symbol of firefighters. A native New Yorker, Fuller agreed to do the design free of charge, working alongside landscape designers, engineers, and planners, who volunteered their time and expertise for the cause. The segment was left standing at its full height to symbolize Americans standing strong after the attack, though it is bent from the extreme heat it survived. Weighing approximately 10 tons, the dark red beam was transported from New York City, draped in American flags and greeted by residents with a motorcade of fire trucks, motorcycles, and police.

The events of 9/11 were an orchestrated series of attacks using four hijacked commercial passenger airliners to crash into the World Trade Center towers, the Pentagon, and a failed Washington, DC attack that ended in a crashing in Pennsylvania. It was the single deadliest terrorist attack in human history and the deadliest-ever incident for first responders in the United States. The Palm Beach Gardens 9/11 Memorial was dedicated in September 2010 and acts as a place for people to mourn, reflect, connect, and pay their respects. The memorial is free and is equally stunning in both daylight and when lit in the evening.

09.11.01 Memorial Plaza

Address 5089 Northlake Boulevard, Palm Beach Gardens, FL 33418, www.pbgfl.com |
Getting there From I-95: Take exit 77 and drive west on Northlake Boulevard about one
mile. Fire Station 3 and parking lot are on the right. | **Hours** Unrestricted | **Tip** Mark Fuller
has created over a dozen pieces of art in the area, including *Butterfly* at PGA Commons
(5100 PGA Boulevard, Palm Beach Gardens, www.pgacommons.com).

2 Blueline Surf & Paddle

Paddle the Jupiter Waterway

For a truly memorable experience on the North County waterways, visit Blueline Surf & Paddle in the heart of Jupiter Inlet Village and rent a stand-up paddleboard or kayak. An area that exudes the personality of this cozy surf town with its breezy palm trees and vibrant venues, the village also provides various drop-in points for these popular modes of transportation along the coastline. Servicing the beach lovers of the area, Blueline is a locals' hub for watersport needs and also caters to visiting enthusiasts looking to try their hand at surfing the glistening whitecaps or fishing the deep blue.

Opened in 2010, Blueline is reflective of the surf community it serves with its laid-back, welcoming, and water-centric atmosphere. The work of Adam and Katy Whittington, Blueline began when stand-up paddleboarding, or "SUP," caught Adam's eye. It was a newer concept gaining popularity out of Hawaii, and there wasn't a large local market for paddleboard sales yet. Adam saw an opportunity and became a wholesaler for the East Coast. Katy's retail background led to a boutique storefront rather than a standard distribution warehouse, and the concept took off. Over time the name grew with branded merchandise and apparel. These days, Blueline is a beloved "Florida Lifestyle" shop. You'll recognize daily operations manager Matt Arensman by his long hair and tanned skin, true to the promise of sun and fun.

Blueline offers activities and excursions including beginner lessons, race leagues, and eco tours, dropping in at Guanabanas just across the street. You can also book private experiences to celebrate a birthday, for corporate team building, to entertain guests, or indulge in a SUP yoga session. Their inventory of equipment, apparel, and accessories available for rental or sale appeals to locals and visitors alike, small kids and senior citizens.

Address 997 Florida A1A, Jupiter, FL 33458, +1 (561) 744-7474, www.bluelinesurf.com | Getting there From I-95: Take exit 87A and drive east on Indiantown Road for about four miles. Turn left on US Highway 1. Turn right on A1A North. Store and parking on the left. | Hours Sun–Thu 9am–7pm, Fri & Sat 9am–8pm | Tip Dine al fresco under the tiki or an umbrella at Guanabanas for a laid-back, hometown experience (960 N Highway A1A, Jupiter, www.guanabanas.com).

3_ The Brewhouse Gallery

A cultural hub of music, murals, and mash

Lake Park began as Kelsey City, named for pioneer Harry Seymour Kelsey, who developed the area for the working class of Palm Beach. Once the owner of the most land in the county, Kelsey established much of the area's infrastructure before the Hurricane of 1928 and financial depression let to the majority buyout of the town. Fast forward to 2014 and the opening of an establishment that would become the catalyst for its revival.

A. J. Brockman never planned to be a gallery owner, nor did he intend to own a theater or brewery. Born with spinal muscular atrophy, he found himself in a wheelchair before the age of three. In middle school, his passion for art was ignited, but by high school, his ability to use his hands had declined. He found graphic design as a path to continue his craft and earn a living. But after a few years in the corporate world, Brockman stepped back to focus on creating fine art. He realized there was a cultural gap to fill and set out to open a space he believed the community needed: The Brewhouse Gallery.

The business thrived, but when the landlord decided to sell the property, Brockman was left with the decision to take over the shopping center and adjoining historic Kelsey Theater, or leave its fate to chance and potential destruction. He took on the challenge, garnered the city's support, built a community around the venue, and in the process commissioned the longest continuous mural in South Florida, measuring over 900 feet.

The Brewhouse Gallery is an art gallery designed to support local artists, while creating a social house of creatives and craft beer lovers. The interior walls are constantly revolving, as artists rent commission-free "gallery space" to sell their artwork. The space takes on the mood of the day with laptops propped open during the afternoons and crowds gathering for intimate musical performances in the evenings.

Address 720 Park Avenue, Lake Park, FL 33403, +1 (561) 469-8930,
www.brewhousegallery.com | Getting there From I-95: Take exit 77 and drive east
on Northlake Boulevard. Turn right on 10th Street. Turn left in Park Avenue. Gallery
and parking on the right. | Hours Wed–Fri 3pm–noon, Sat noon–midnight,
Sun noon–10pm | Tip Catch a show at the Kelsey Theater, which holds 300 to
400 people and features musical acts and performances (700 Park Avenue, Lake Park,
www.thekelseytheater.com).

4__ Cato's Bridge
Action below the bridge

When venturing from Jupiter Island to the mainland, motorists will find themselves crossing the CR 707 or Beach Road Bridge. But to locals, this structure and the narrow beach along the shore beneath it are considered "Cato's Bridge." Avon Charles Cato tended the bridge for over three decades. At one point, he lived in a white house just beside it with his family before his death in 1969. A place of nostalgic appeal for many, the bridge has long been a meeting place for friends to rope swing, snorkel, paddleboard, and barbeque.

Much of the allure of this swimming hole stems from its location between the freshwater Loxahatchee River and saltwater Intracoastal Waterway just off the Jupiter Inlet. This blending of salinity levels breeds a diverse commingling of marine life, making this a hotspot for snorkelers. The picturesque blue water shifts with the tides and allows boats to anchor along the shore as divers explore the western side, albeit in short spurts for safety.

The shallower east side is a great spot for lounging on the shore and dipping your toes in the water, while land explorers take the trail on the south side to venture to Hammock Hangout. There you can find large wooden posts installed to create a "bring your own hammock" nature hideaway.

Cato's Bridge is quintessential Jupiter, with its local nickname, boat access, nature-centric activities, and laid-back vibes. Many have earned their stripes jumping from the bridge – at their own risk – into the clear water below. When you visit, remember to bring a mask and snorkel for the opportunity to see a variety of fish, manatees, or even a shark. But be sure to pay attention to boat traffic, changing tides, and strong currents that can be potentially dangerous, especially for younger swimmers. The varying species of marine life cycle with the weather and water temperatures, creating endless sights to see and days to enjoy under Cato's beloved bridge.

Address S Beach Road, Tequesta, FL 33469 | Getting there From I-95: Take exit 87A and drive east on Indiantown Road. Turn left on Alt A1A N. Continue onto S Beach Road. The bridge is straight ahead. Parking nearby. | Hours Unrestricted | Tip Shop for ocean-inspired homewares and accessories at the nearby Nautical But Nice Trading Company boutique (265 S US Highway 1, Tequesta, www.nauticalbutnicetc.com).

5   Dog Beach

Unleash the salty hounds of Jupiter Beach

South Florida is known far and wide for its beautiful coastline. From their soft, warm sands to their sparkling blue waters, the beaches of Palm Beach County can be found covered in sunbathers, surfers, tiny sandcastle builders, and, in Jupiter, salty dogs. Starting at marker number 25 and heading north to marker 59 is the area known as "Dog Beach." This strip of sand is a leash-free, beachfront dog park, inviting owners to lounge or play with their canine companions.

Since 1989, Jupiter Beach has been considered dog-friendly, and in 1994, the not-for-profit organization Friends of Jupiter Beach (FJB) began volunteering to keep it pristine. Through monthly beach cleanups, community events, and initiatives like sanitary bag dispensers for pet owners' use, FJB has worked to remove thousands of pounds of garbage, taught etiquette to maintain good standing with the Town of Jupiter, and acted as ambassadors for the beach to ensure that everyone respects its environmental importance.

At shower number 33 at Dog Beach, you'll find "Kite Beach," a popular area for kitesurfers. On a breezy day, the sky is filled with colorful kites carrying riders upwards of 10 mph along the waves below. It's all visible from the pier at Juno Beach, and you can watch the vibrant canvases dance through the clouds. On calmer days, stand-up paddleboarders take to the waves with skimboarders along the break. Just up Ocean Boulevard at beach access number 51 is one of the most iconic entries to Jupiter Beach. You will walk through a tunnel of seagrapes before emerging onto the shoreline.

Jupiter Beach is home to various points of interest for beachgoers. A popular locale for cyclists and joggers, friends and families, there are miles of oceanfront to enjoy. County parks like Carlin Park and Ocean Cay Park give reprieve from the sun with pavilions, restroom facilities, and showers.

Address 2188 Marcinski Road, Jupiter, FL 33477, www.jupiter.fl.us | Getting there From I-95: Take exit 83 and drive east on Donald Ross Boulevard. Turn left on US Highway 1. Turn right on Marcinski Road. Ocean Cay Park and parking will be on the right. Beach street parking is available. | Hours Unrestricted | Tip Known by locals as "No Name Beach," Pier-less Beach Park is located in Juno Beach just south of the pier and popular tourist spots. Due to its less obvious entrance and limited parking, this public access point provides a semi-private experience (10 Mercury Road, Juno Beach).

6 DuBois Pioneer House
The house on the hill

At the north end of the county lies DuBois Park, a one-stop glimpse into the past and present of Jupiter. Sparkling turquoise waters lure snorkelers into the lagoon, among the mangroves, and through the winding surroundings of the park. On land, history overlooks the modern bustle through the windows of the DuBois Pioneer House.

Henry "Harry" DuBois was one of the area's prominent pioneers at the turn of the twentieth century. During his time, he hauled building materials via sailboat to assist with the construction of Palm Beach. He planted pineapple trees along the inlet and harvested bee aviaries, becoming one of the state's first commercial beekeepers. In 1898, he and his wife hired Charlie Carlin to build a "house on the hill," a formidable home built on a mound of shells and ancient Native American refuse.

Carlin was the son of Charles Carlin, Captain of the US Life Saving Station, where DuBois had served several years guarding the lives of passing boaters and saving those from shipwrecks. The coveted mound has since provided archeological insight into Jupiter, with artifacts dating back thousands of years and telling the tales of the land. The 14x28' foot house still stands today, one of the only original homesteads in the area, now featuring a second story and open for tours. Also on the site is the Pineapple House, a small, 1800s shack that has housed pineapples and guests alike, and that is believed to be the oldest frame structure still standing in Jupiter.

Visit DuBois Park for its variety of outdoor activities, from kayaking and fishing, to playgrounds and picnicking. From the jetty, you can watch boats coming into the inlet, a notoriously difficult pass with hidden shoal builds that create unpredictable wave patterns. You can swim, snorkel, and lounge in the lagoon, but beware of the inlet's dangerous currents.

Address 19075 DuBois Road, Jupiter, FL 33477, +1 (561) 966-6600, discover.pbcgov.org |
Getting there From I-95: Take exit 87A and drive east on Indiantown Road for about five
miles. Turn left on N Highway A1A / Ocean Boulevard, then right on Jupiter Beach Road.
Turn left on DuBois Road, then right as DuBois Road turns into DuBois Park. Park and
parking are on the left. | Hours Daily dawn−dusk | Tip Enjoy a tasty breakfast or lunch
at the Lazy Loggerhead Café in the nearby Carlin Park (6 Van Kessel Parkway, Jupiter,
www.lazyloggerheadcafe.com).

7__Gas Station Dumpster Art
Juno Beach roadmap at the Mobil loo

Behind the Mobil gas station at the fork in the road leading into Juno Beach, and right next to the bathrooms, is a vibrant mural featuring a mileage sign for popular destinations near and far. The artwork is fitting, as the station is often used as a directional landmark for those headed north on US Highway 1 or veering right to coast up Ocean Drive.

Rarely do gas station facilities get photographed and shared on social media and travel websites like this one has – repeatedly – over the years. And with mosaic-tiled bathroom walls, the antique goods for sale at the Juno Beach Mart inside the gas station, the vintage soda machine, and the outdoor dog bar, there is a lot more to do here than pump gas.

The hidden gem road sign mural graces the door of the dumpster and was painted by local artist Karen Flint. The arrows point travelers in the direction of the popular Juno Beach pier just 2.1 miles away and further north to the iconic Jupiter Lighthouse at 6.1 miles away, and it gives some perspective with Nassau, Bahamas just a short 209 miles away. The location of the colorful painting is in stark contrast to other works by the same artist. Flint is an accomplished artist with a portfolio of awards, solo exhibitions, and shows. The Fashion Institute of Technology graduate has created privately commissioned originals alongside her fine art and public murals. So the chance to see her talents protecting yesterday's garbage is a surprising treat.

The station itself is a popular stopping point for beachgoers, locals, and visitors alike. Whether motorists are filling up, grabbing a cold drink, or stocking the cooler with ice, the convenience store offers an old school, small town feel. Patrons can peruse antique finds, pose alongside a classic Ford, or pick up a pack of gum. Just don't forget to use the loo before heading on to the next destination.

Address 12750 US-1, Juno Beach, FL 33408, +1 (561) 622-6885 | **Getting there** From I-95: Take exit 79A and drive east on PGA Boulevard. Turn left on US Highway 1. Gas station is on the right with parking. Bathrooms are on the east side. | **Hours** Unrestricted | **Tip** Just around the corner is Palm Beach Sandals, offering a selection of Jackie Kennedy-inspired, open-toe footwear (12832 US-1, Juno Beach, www.palmbeachsandals.com).

8 Hidden WWII Memorial

Where two heroes intersect

Our Freedom, Our Fortune, Their Sacrifice are the words engraved on the memorial to the World War II soldiers, whose names grace the street signs at the corner of Donald Ross Road and Ellison Wilson Road. On the southwest corner of the intersection is a three-foot monument that few people ever notice. Both Wilson and Ross lost their lives in battle during the Ardennes Counteroffensive, a major German campaign against the Allies that moved along the Western Front.

Ellison Wilson was a tank gunner for the Third Armored Division during World War II. He was killed in action at the age of 36 on December 28, 1944 in Belgium, when his tank struck a mine. Originally from Tennessee, Wilson moved to the area in 1923, when he was 15. One of eight siblings, he was a member of the family that founded Lake Park, previously known as Kelsey City. His mother was the beloved principal of Lake Park Elementary School, Marjorie Ross. The Wilson family farm, built by his father Frank, ran along the Intracoastal and Prosperity Farms Road, but it was destroyed in the Hurricane of 1928, along with much of the Prosperity settlement.

Lieutenant Donald Alexander Ross was awarded a Silver Star after leading the Army's 191st Tank Battalion in North Africa. He died on December 18, 1944 in Germany during the Battle of the Bulge. He was 24 and the first Lake Park resident to be killed in action in World War II. Ross had moved to the area in 1928 and grew up on the waterways of Lake Park and Singer Island. People often mistakenly think that the road is named after another Donald Ross, the famous golf course designer of the nearby Seminole Golf Club and Gulfstream Golf Club in Delray Beach. However the true namesake died within days of his fellow local war hero, their legacies now honored together on this stone. Next time you pass by, stop and remember these courageous men.

Address Corner of Donald Ross Road and Ellison Wilson Road, Juno Beach, FL 33408 | **Getting there** From I-95: Take exit 83 and drive east on Donald Ross Road about 3.5 miles. Cross the bridge and park near the intersection of Ellison Wilson Road. Monument is on the southwest corner of the intersection. | **Hours** Unrestricted | **Tip** Visit the Delray Beach Golf Course, one of several designed by Donald James Ross in the Palm Beaches (2200 Highland Avenue, Delray Beach, www.delraybeachgolfclub.com).

9 _ JFK's Island Bunker

Snooze on Peanut Island

At the center of the Port of Palm Beach lies a man-made land formation called Peanut Island, or "pnut" to the locals. Constructed in 1918 during the dredging of the Lake Worth Inlet, the island's name is a mystery to many. While some assume it is named for its diminutive size or possibly its shape, the name actually stemmed from a plan to use the island as a shipping terminal for peanut oil in the 1940s. The concept never came to fruition, but the name stuck. Today, the island stands at the center of a popular boaters' destination with the daily appearance of the nearby sandbar.

Since its creation and subsequent dredging, the island has grown to become home to an 80-acre park accessed by boat, kayak, or water taxi. The park features 20 campsites, where you can take in the Palm Beach air while grilling out during the day or camping overnight. A perimeter walking trail allows easy access around the formation, and you can look for the historic Coast Guard building on the south side of the island.

During the Cold War, a secret bunker was implanted for John F. Kennedy (see ch. 57), who frequented Palm Beach with his family. The bunker sat for years as a museum-like time capsule, providing a peek into its historic relics, papers, and the presidential seal emblazoned on the bunker's floor. While it's still a destination for visitors to view from the outside, the interior of "Detachment Hotel" is now closed to the public.

During the day, the island is open to visitors to access via the waterway at Riviera Beach Marina. As the tide recedes, the sandbar to the north of the island becomes visible and becomes a hangout for friends and families looking for fun in the sun. Overnight camping requires a permit that is fairly inexpensive and provides access to barbecue grills along the beach. Drinking and pets are allowed within the camp area, and tents are required for sleeping.

Address Lake Worth Inlet, 6500 Peanut Island Road, Riviera Beach, FL 33404, +1 (561) 845-4445, discover.pbcgov.org/parks/Locations/Peanut-Island.aspx | Getting there From I-95: Take exit 76 and drive east on Blue Heron Boulevard. Turn right on Broadway Avenue then left on E 13th Street. Riviera Beach Marina overlooks Peanut Island and offers boat services. | Hours Dawn–dusk (unless camping) | Tip If you don't have access to a boat, book the shuttle boat service to Peanut Island from Riviera Beach Marina leaving every 20 minutes (200 E 13th Street, Riviera Beach, www.peanutislandshuttleboat.com).

10 Juno Beach Pier Sunrise
Picture perfect morning rays

A 990-foot causeway extending from Juno Beach Park into the Atlantic Ocean, the Juno Beach Pier is known for its stunning sunrises and saltwater fishing. Managed by Loggerhead Marinelife Center, the pier is divided into thirds for popular catches with the first section yielding fish like snook and flounder; the second section for pompano, mackerel, and bluefish; and the end of the pier is grounds for cobia and kingfish. Fishermen can rent poles, purchase bait, pay fees, and grab a snack at the Juno Beach Pier House at the pier's entry.

The current pier was opened in 1999, but there is greater history behind it. The original Juno Beach Pier was built in 1949 at just over half the size and was privately owned. In 1977, Wally and Penny Sheltz purchased the pier and maintained a small business to cover the expense of maintenance. Over time, officials decided the pier was a safety hazard, and after the strong winds and high waves of a 1984 storm damaged much of the structure, the Sheltzs were required to dismantle what little remained. A petition was submitted to Palm Beach County commissioners and presented to the State of Florida, and they approved the rebuilding of a new pier, which is the one that stands there now. The replacement, a multi-million-dollar plank walkway, rests on metal and concrete columns with shaded stops and fish cleaning stations leading out to its T-shaped end.

The pier is a much admired subject for local photographers and landmark for visitors. Below the pier, stretching north and south along Ocean Drive, are the beautiful sands of Juno Beach. There is a steady stream of beachgoers from just before sunrise to sunset each day. The pier offers a shady reprieve during the high heat of the day. Within a short radius of the pier are lifeguarded areas for swimming and surfing, making it a popular locale on beach weather days.

Address 14775 US-1, Juno Beach, FL 33408, +1 (561) 855-6185, www.marinelife.org | Getting there From I-95: Take exit 83 and drive east on Donald Ross Road about four miles. Turn left onto Ocean Drive. Pier located on the right. Public parking lot on left. | Hours Daily dawn–dusk | Tip Pick up beach gear at Locals Surf Shop just across the street in Bluffs Square Shoppes (4050 S US Highway 1, Unit 304, Jupiter, www.localssurfshop.com).

11 Jupiter Donut
Where donut dreams come true

Jupiter Donut has been churning out their popular fried dough confections from their flagship Center Street shop since 2013, known for their fresh ingredients, unique flavors, and photo-worthy decorations. Customers typically arrive ready for a line out the door. But becoming one of the most popular doughnut shops in South Florida didn't necessarily require knowing anything about doughnuts.

Owner Adam Jones and his family were in the market for a new business venture, when his brother mentioned a popular doughnut shop in the heart of Jupiter. As none of them knew anything about making doughnuts, he asked if he could work and train under their bakers. After a couple of months, the owners offered him the option to purchase their operation versus starting his own competing business, and a deal was struck. The family decided to rebrand with a local name, retro flair, larger doughnuts, and innovative toppings.

The concept of Jupiter Donuts became crowds at the door, sellout weekends, and multiple locations throughout the state. Bakers arrive at midnight, decorators follow a few hours later, and the doors open at 6am. Hundreds of doughnuts are made and "dressed" each day, and the shop stays open until 1pm or till the donuts are sold out. The business has remained close-knit – each new location is owned and operated by a family member.

You'll be greeted by a wall display stocked with over 40 flavors of doughnuts to choose from, including classics like Glazed or Boston Cream, colorfully topped Fruity Pebbles or M&Ms, and local favorites like Samoa, inspired by the Girl Scout cookie. Seasonal varieties and monthly specials rotate among Pumpkin, Key Lime, and treats like the Kronut and Cinnamon Roll. Breakfast sandwiches, bagels, and croissants are available for those looking for a savory option, as well as their own unique blend of coffee.

Address 141 Center Street, Jupiter, FL 33458, +1 (561) 741-5290, www.jupiterdonuts.com | Getting there From I-95: Take exit 87A and drive east on Indiantown Road. Turn left onto Center Street. Upper Crust Jupiter Donuts and parking will be located on the left. | Hours Daily 6am–1pm | Tip For a savory holed breakfast treat, head to locally owned and operated Bagel Boyz, also open for lunch (5430 Military Trail, Unit 80, Jupiter, www.bagel-boyz.com).

12   Jupiter Inlet Lighthouse

The oldest building shines a light on Jupiter

A historic landmark and local treasure, the Jupiter Lighthouse is the oldest building in Palm Beach County. Dating back to the 1800s, it was designed by George Gordon Meade who later went on to famously defeat General Robert E. Lee at the Battle of Gettysburg. Captain Edward Yorke completed construction and the first lighting occurred on July 10, 1860. In 2008, Congress bestowed federally protected status on the Jupiter Inlet Lighthouse Outstanding Natural Area to preserve its biodiversity and history. With views of four different bodies of water – the Atlantic Ocean, Indian River, Loxahatchee River, and Jupiter Inlet – the iconic red lighthouse stands 108-feet tall, and its light is visible from 24 nautical miles away. Located on one of only three federally designated Outstanding Natural Areas in the US, the 120-acre site is the only one east of California.

The location of the lighthouse dates back to the ancient Native Americans of the area, who used the point where the Indian River intersects with the Jupiter Inlet as a meeting place. A non-agricultural people, the Jobe and Jeaga tribes were known for their ability to travel the waterways of Florida in carved canoes, fishing and hunting game. Various run-ins between the tribes and exploring Spaniards were documented, including the 1696 capture of Jonathan Dickinson and his family and crew. Dickinson described a large shell mound where the Jeaga tribe lived, which now rests partially beneath the 1898 Pioneer Home in DuBois Park (see ch. 6). Artifacts dating as far back as 5000 BC have been found within the mound.

Visitors can climb the stairs of the lighthouse and learn its history in the on-site museum located in a restored World War II building operated by the Loxahatchee River Historical Society. A handful of events are held at the lighthouse throughout the year, giving ticket holders an opportunity to experience the grounds in new and fascinating ways.

Address 500 Captain Armour's Way, Jupiter, FL 33469, +1 (561) 747-8380, www.jupiterlighthouse.org | **Getting there** From I-95: Take exit 87A and drive east on Indiantown Road. Turn left on Center Street. Turn left on Alt A1A. Turn right on Captain Armour's Way. Lighthouse and parking on left. | **Hours** See website for hours | **Tip** Enjoy a view of the lighthouse dining across the inlet at U-Tiki Beach (1095 N Highway A1A, Jupiter, www.utikibeach.com).

13 Jupiter Ridge

Bird watching along longest Intracoastal shoreline

Hiding along the US Highway 1 corridor, between Donald Ross Road and Indiantown Road, is the longest shoreline along the Intracoastal at Jupiter Ridge Natural Area. Over 250 acres of scrub, marsh, and swamp ecosystems exist within the preserve that stretches along over 7,000 feet of water frontage. A massive $23-million undertaking involving a $11-million match from the state of Florida enabled the securing of the land to protect the ecosystems and wildlife living within.

A stop along the Great Florida Birding and Wildlife Trail (GFBWT), there have been over 120 species of birds sighted within the natural area, including rare birds of prey, owls, warblers, and wading birds. While some are found year-round, others make their appearance during seasonal migrations. The native Florida scrub-jay can be found on the property – look for its thick beak, long tail, and beautiful shade of blue with white and gray markings. This vulnerable species is the only bird that lives exclusively in the state of Florida and is a perfect example of why protected shrub areas are needed. The South Region of the GFBWT spans from Martin County down into Monroe County and the Florida Keys, with numerous points of interest along the way, 18 of which are located in Palm Beach County. Beyond the birds, the natural area provides a safe environment for marine life, like manatees, vegetation (including mangroves), and restorative oyster reefs.

Come explore the area and partake in non-invasive activities, like bird watching, nature walks, and photography. There are over two miles across three hiking trails. The only paved pathway is the Little Blue Heron Trail, so dress accordingly for walking on sand. Climb an observation platform for a view of the shoreline and wildlife. You can get here by small boats and watercraft by pulling up to the popular Ski Beach.

Address 1800 S US Highway 1, Jupiter, FL 33477, discover.pbcgov.org | Getting there
From I-95: Take exit 79A and drive east on PGA Boulevard. Turn left onto US-1 North,
then left onto Oceanside Terrace. Jupiter Ridge Natural Area and parking are on the left. |
Hours Daily dawn–dusk | Tip Just down the road from Jupiter Ridge is Frenchman's Forest,
a nature preserve that provides habitat for rare and endangered animal and plant species
(12201 Prosperity Farms Road, Palm Beach Gardens).

14 Loxahatchee Battlefield

Burial grounds within Riverbend Park

Within Riverbend Park is the 64-acre Loxahatchee Battlefield Park. A serene setting with expansive greenery, a winding river, and hidden wildlife within the cypress canopies, this idyllic space was the site of the last two major battles of the Second Seminole War (1835–1842). Visitors to the park can explore the waterway by kayak, trails by bike, or enjoy a picnic under a pavilion. A gateway to the Loxahatchee River, this area has been a settling place for thousands of years and became a point of combat that would turn it into a Native American burial ground.

On January 15, 1838, at the direction of Major General Thomas Jesup, Lieutenant Levin M. Powell led an inexperienced Navy's Waterborne Everglades Expeditionary Unit into what became known as Powell's Battle. His unit entered the southwest fork of the river and marched west, where they were surprised by Seminole warriors under Chiefs Tuskegee and Halleck Hadjo. The small group of less than 100 soldiers was overcome by the attack, suffering considerable casualties. Joseph W. Johnston was commended for his stepping in to avoid what could have been a massacre, but it was still a resounding loss.

Nine days later, on January 24, 1838 a second battle was brought to the Seminole people, this time with over 1,000 men and General Jesup at the helm. Joined by the Tennessee Volunteers under Major William Lauderdale, Colonel William Harney and his cavalry out-maneuvered the Seminoles, forcing their retreat into the swamp. The US Forces' casualties were low, although the General was wounded. Washington, DC denied a request to allow the Seminoles to remain in the Everglades, and they were instead detained at Fort Jupiter. Annual battle reenactments and preservationist tours are now hosted in the park to commemorate what is known as "the longest, costliest and bloodiest Indian war ever fought."

Address 9060 W Indiantown Road, Jupiter, FL 3347, +1 (561) 743-6419, www.loxahatcheebattlefield.com | Getting there From I-95: Take exit 87B and drive west for about seven miles. Turn left into park. Outdoor center and parking on the left. | Hours Daily dusk–dawn | Tip Memorials for the Second Seminole War can also be found nearby at Jonathan Dickinson State Park (16450 SE Federal Highway, Hobe Sound, www.jdstatepark.com).

15 — Lyn St. James Crash Site
Making a fiery entrance at PBIR

Known for two decades as Moroso Motorsports Park, Palm Beach International Raceway opened in 1964. In 1969, the raceway hosted a historic rock festival, featuring performances by artists such as Janis Joplin, The Rolling Stones, and Jefferson Airplane. Just 10 years later in 1979, sports car and Indy 500 racer Lyn St. James made her professional debut at the facility. The spectacle ended when she lost control of her Ford Pinto street car and crashed into a swamp off the track, escaping the vehicle just before it sank.

Lyn St. James, born Evelyn Gene Cornwall, began her racing career late in life. She was the first woman to win a solo professional road race at Watkins Glen in New York in 1985 before becoming the first woman to compete full-time on the Indy circuit in 1988. In 1992, she became just the second woman to race at Indy in the Indianapolis 500, coming in 11th out of 33 racers.

Her love of cars originated from her mother, who suffered from polio and found driving an empowering activity. An active athlete, her interest in racing began when she attended races with her friends and became her passion after a trip to the Indianapolis 500. Despite her early accident at Moroso, she enjoyed success until her retirement in 2001.

Today, the state-of-the-art facility boasts a quarter-mile IHRA-sanctioned drag strip, 2.2-mile 10-turn road course, 7/10-mile kart track and mud bog. The Palm Beach International Raceway Drag Strip is one of only six tracks in the country built completely from concrete. Using advanced technology for the lighting, scoring, and timing, along with the increased stability and evenness, it is a well-respected track in racing. In 2019, at the age of 87, "Big Daddy" Don Garlits set a new world speed record for an electric dragster on the smooth surface. The raceway hosts events, races, and a driving school, where you can expand your own skills.

Address 17047 Bee Line Highway, Jupiter, FL 33478, +1 (561) 622-1400, www.racepbir.com | Getting there From I-95: Take exit 79B and drive west on PGA Boulevard for about six miles. Turn right onto FL-710W for about 8.5 miles. Raceway is on the right. | Hours See website for events schedule | Tip Car enthusiasts can see an array of vintage cars at Ragtops in West Palm Beach (2025 N Dixie Highway, West Palm Beach, www.ragtopsmotorcars.com).

16 MacArthur's Banyan Tree
A living tribute to a founding father

Motorists fighting rush hour on Northlake Boulevard may not notice the 80-year-old banyan tree at its intersection with MacArthur Boulevard. The expansive tree, with its pillar-esque prop roots and sprawling limbs, stands as a symbol of John D. MacArthur's commitment to creating the landscape of the city of Palm Beach Gardens.

In 1961, MacArthur had the 75-ton tree moved approximately five miles from its original home, where its roots were damaging a nearby house. On the day of the transplant, after six months of painstakingly planning the move, the tree hit some railway signal lines above the road, closing crossing gates for eight miles. Next, a cable snapped, and the giant tree dropped onto the train tracks. All in all, over 1,000 hours of manpower went into the chaotic relocation before the tree settled into its new home.

John D. MacArthur was the Palm Beach Gardens equivalent of Henry Flagler on the island (see ch. 73). An American rags-to-riches businessman, philanthropist, and billionaire, he made his fortune in insurance, and purchased over 2,000 acres of Palm Beach Gardens for $5.5 million in the mid-1950s. MacArthur was known to work from a small coffee shop in the Colonnades Beach Hotel on Singer Island, where he and his wife Catherine lived modestly in an apartment overlooking Lake Worth. MacArthur died in 1978 at the age of 81 and as one of the wealthiest men in America. While he left behind a charitable foundation and has posthumously given almost a thousand "genius grants," MacArthur's legacy has seen much scrutiny due to his cunning attitude in business and life.

A member of the Ficus species, banyans are the world's largest tree in terms of area covered – the record holder shades almost five acres in its native India. Thriving in tropical and subtropical climates, they are a symbolic natural element to the state of Florida and can survive for centuries.

Address Corner of Northlake Boulevard and MacArthur Boulevard, Palm Beach Gardens, FL 33403 | Getting there From I-95: Take exit 77 and drive east on Northlake Boulevard for about a mile. Turn left on MacArthur Boulevard. Tree is centered in the road. | Hours Unrestricted | Tip Camp out at John D. MacArthur State Park, the only state park in the county, with grounds and cabins available for short-term rental and snorkel the Anastasia Limestone Rock Reef (10900 Jack Nicklaus Drive, North Palm Beach, www.macarthurbeach.org).

17 — Maltz Jupiter Theatre
From student to star-studded

Originally the Burt Reynolds Dinner Theatre, the regional Maltz Jupiter Theatre was brought back to life in the early 2000s hosting local and national productions. Rich with history, in its heyday the Burt Reynolds Theatre welcomed more celebrities than any other Palm Beach County venue. Sally Field ushered in the inaugural season in 1979 and was followed with performances by Carol Burnett, Farrah Fawcett, Martin Sheen, and Sarah Jessica Parker, among the star-studded casts. Reynolds himself performed and directed a handful of shows, even as one of the biggest stars in Hollywood.

Burt "Buddy" Reynolds was raised in Palm Beach County and became a beloved icon of the area. He attended Palm Beach High School, now A. W. Dreyfoos Schools of the Arts, earning a scholarship to Florida State University for football. A career-ending knee injury brought him home to Palm Beach Junior College and set his new path towards acting into motion. His role in *Deliverance* proved to be his breakout performance which led to a decades-long career in movies. He won several Golden Globes, was nominated for an Academy Award, and received a star on the Hollywood Walk of Fame. Through all of his success, he chose to keep this little beach town his home. Reynolds is credited by many for putting Jupiter on the map as an integral part of the community. He shot movies at local locations, like the bridge jump scene in *Smokey the Bandit II*. Reynolds passed away in 2018 at the age of 82, sparking a local outpouring of love and respect for the fallen actor.

Named in honor of founding members and generous supporters Milton and Tamar Maltz, the theater as it stands today was resurrected in 2001. A not-for-profit entity, it has been supported by volunteers, grants, and box office sales. The theater provides educational opportunities for aspiring actors and has grown to be the largest regional theater in the state.

Address 1001 E Indiantown Road, Jupiter, FL 33477, +1 (561) 575-2223, www.jupitertheatre.org | Getting there From I-95: Take exit 87A and drive east on Indiantown Road for about three miles. Theater and parking is located on the right. | Hours See website for event schedule | Tip Grill a hamburger, play in the horseshoe pits, and explore the aquariums at the Loxahatchee River Center in the nearby Burt Reynolds Park (805 N US Highway 1, Jupiter, www.jupiter.fl.us).

18   Munyon Island

Hygeia on the lesser-known island

Originally called *Nuctsachoo* by the Seminole tribe, or "Pelican Island," Munyon Island is part of John D. MacArthur Beach State Park (see ch. 16). Originally a narrow, 15-acre island, it has been expanded through dredging and is a popular destination for kayakers and boaters. But long before its 1955 acquisition, the island was home to Rodgers, a man who lived in a tent on the land in the late 1800s. The Pitts family purchased the land, built a home, and developed a horticultural area.

Just after 1900, James Munyon, famous for his homeopathic remedies, purchased the island and set up a post office. When the mail service was transferred to Mangonia Park, he established a five-story hotel. Hotel Hygeia, named for the goddess of good health, was marketed as a retreat, where guests were invited to bathe in a "fountain of youth" and sip "Dr. Munyon's Paw-Paw Elixir," a fermented papaya juice. Not long after a fire claimed the hotel, Harry Seymour Kelsey purchased the island in a larger deal that included a resort that never came to fruition.

The land was eventually dredged, tripling the island's size, before it was acquired by MacArthur. Eventually, it was donated to the State of Florida and and became a welcome and important addition to the park. Wildlife enthusiasts enjoy the many birds that grace the island and manatees that can be found drifting among over 100,000 wetland plants during season.

You can reach the island's dock by boat. Kayakers can explore the estuaries and pull up onto the sand. A boardwalk winds around the island, which is also dotted with picnic pavilions and natural trails. If you'd like to visit the area without venturing onto the water, you can drive onto the state park for a picnic or a stroll. Enjoy a variety of activities both on land and under water with year-round programming, including guided nature walks and concerts.

Address 10900 Jack Nicklaus Drive, North Palm Beach, FL 33408, +1 (561) 624-6950, www.macarthurbeach.org | **Getting there** From I-95: Take exit 79AB and drive east on PGA Boulevard. Continue onto Jack Nicklaus Drive. Park entrance and parking is located on the left. | **Hours** Daily 8am–dusk | **Tip** Venture further south on Singer Island to Paradise Coffee and Gifts for a cup of joe or knickknack (1283 Blue Heron Boulevard, Singer Island, paradise-coffee-and-gifts.business.site).

19 Perry Como's Final Gig

Burial on the county line at Riverside Memorial Park

Pulling into the entrance of Riverside Memorial Park, you'll be met with a lush landscape of greenery, tree canopies, and rows of vibrant flowers left by loved ones. The cemetery features vaults, tombstones, and mausoleums with seating for contemplation and remembrance. Rich with history, the over 30-acre park is home to the graves of television host Michael Douglas, Major League Baseball Hall of Famer Gary "The Kid" Carter, and Perry Como.

Pierino "Perry" Como was a multifaceted talent, whose career spanned half a century and crossed over from radio to television. Born in Pennsylvania, Como showed an interest in music from a young age. He learned several instruments and worked as a gigging musician and performer before signing with RCA. A crooner in style, his greatest hits include "And I Love You So" and "Catch a Falling Star." A baritone, Como was known as "Mr. C" and garnered three stars on the Hollywood Walk of Fame for television, music, and radio.

Como's crossover into television came by way of his variety show, one of the first of its kind and one of the longest-running shows in its history. Stepping back from the limelight, Como continued his widely popular Christmas specials, which were filmed in several countries throughout the years. In 2001, Como passed away in his sleep, just less than a week before his 89th birthday. He is buried in section five of Riverside's Garden of Reflection.

Within Riverside is the original century-old Jupiter Cemetery, which contains the graves of many of the area's leaders. Expanded and manicured by former owner Roy Rood in the 1940s, the burial grounds became part of a sprawling park. The overall make-up of gravesites includes both Catholics and Jews, alongside veterans and celebrities. You can come here for a calming stroll, or ride your bike among the large oak trees, angelic statues, and monuments.

Address 19351 SE County Line Road, Tequesta, FL 33469, +1 (561) 747-1100 | Getting there From I-95: Take exit 78B and drive east on Indiantown Road. Turn left on Alt A1A, then left on N Old Dixie Highway. Turn left on SE County Line Road. The park is on the right. | Hours Daily dawn–dusk | Tip Enjoy tacos, margaritas, and yard games at the vibrant Papichulo Tacos (1556 US-1, Jupiter, www.papichulotacos.com).

20 The Pumphouse
Shaping the waterways of Palm Beach

In the late 1800s, settlers embarked on the massive task of digging a man-made channel in place of the natural waterway at Lake Worth Inlet to create a consistent path for fishing boats. Volunteers succeeded but were met with the challenge of the south side eroding while the north side filled, causing the channel to shift and lose depth. Throughout the early 1900s digs continued, deepening and widening the channel, allowing cargo and passenger ships to pass. The late 1920s proved to be a time of setbacks, but after World War II and into the 1960s the channel was dredged reaching its current 35-foot depth. The channel became the entrance to the Port of Palm Beach, which still requires attention but has also led to the creation of sandy beaches along Palm Beach Shores.

While many have scaled, surfed, and snapped images of the large, oddly-shaped, metal contraption situated on the north side, few know its purpose. Built in 1958, the sand transfer plant, known by locals as the Pumphouse, is used to move sand from Singer Island to Palm Beach to help recreate the natural flow of sand and maintain the channel. It was modeled to transplant approximately 250,000 cubic yards annually. In the 1990s, the plant was shut down due to the transfer pipe rusting through on the ocean floor, but after the pipeline was drilled 15 feet below the bottom of the inlet, the plant was upgraded and continued on.

Despite the lack of parking, Pumphouse is a popular beach hangout with locals fearlessly ignoring danger signs and climbing the tower to jump in the waves below, while surfers paddle alongside looking for swells. The jetty is often sprinkled with fishermen and snorkelers exploring nearby. The sand transfer plant has become a local landmark. It is photographed regularly by local talents like Captain Kimo, featured in drone videos, and used as a backdrop for stunning sunrises.

Address Beach at S Ocean Avenue and Inlet Way, Palm Beach Shores, FL 33404 | Getting there From I-95: Take exit 77 and drive east on Blue Heron Boulevard about three miles. Cross Blue Heron Bridge onto Singer Island. Turn right on Lake Drive. Turn left on Inlet Way. Pumphouse is located on the southeast edge of the beach. | Hours Daily dawn–dusk | Tip Head to Jupiter to enjoy a cup of coffee by Pumphouse Coffee Roasters, named after the local landmark and started by two brothers who grew up climbing that very sand plant (997 N Highway A1A ,Unit B, Jupiter, www.pumphousecoffeeroasters.com).

21 — Sailfish Marina

Catch, eat, or feed the fish

Sailfish Marina is much more than a place to dock a boat. The multi-purpose property hosts a waterfront motel, event venue, restaurant, tiki bar, and marina. The marina has a deep-rooted history in sport fishing dating back to the early 20th century. As sport fishing gained popularity in the early 1900s, Palm Beach and Singer Island became a destination for the fishing community. Old fishing tales may refer to the location as "Bill's Marina" or "Roy's Dock," depending on who owned the property when they reeled in a big one. Since the 1970s, Alexander Dreyfoos has combined multiple properties into what is now Sailfish Marina. Today, the marina is a popular destination, due to its proximity to the Palm Beach Inlet and short jog to the Bahamas.

The warm current of the Gulf Stream creates a food chain just off the coast that greatly benefits nearby boats. As seaweed gathers on the surface, it attracts baitfish, and they bring larger fish from deeper waters. Dockside photographs show catches of hooked marlin and tuna, as well as smiling captains. From the restaurant, you can watch the boats come and go, while fishermen weigh their catches and filet them dockside for dinner. Kids jump at the opportunity to purchase bags of fish food at the bait shop to satiate the jack fish that surround the slips in the "seawall aquarium."

The restaurant features a casual seafood and Caribbean-inspired menu, with weekend brunch buffets and tiki cocktails. Weekly programming includes live music and with annual events, like Bluewater Babes and Lobsterfest, bringing together enthusiasts from throughout the area. Fishing and boating lovers who do not have their own vessel can choose from a selection of captained charters available for day trips and hourly rentals. The Ship Store bait shop beside the restaurant offers merchandise, novelty items, resort wear, and boat gear.

Address 98 Lake Drive, West Palm Beach, FL 33404, +1 (561) 844-1724, www.sailfishmarina.com | **Getting there** From I-95: Take exit 76 to and drive east on Blue Heron Boulevard. Cross over the Blue Heron Bridge. Turn right onto Lake Drive. The marina and parking are on the right. | **Hours** Mon–Fri 7am–9pm, Sat & Sun 6:30am–9pm | **Tip** Just over half a mile away is the Easternmost Point in Florida. Travel south on Lake Drive onto Inlet Way and walk to the southeast corner of the island for a perfect sunrise (Palm Beach Shores).

22 Sea Shell City

Trinkets and treasures from the sea

Family owned and operated since 1969, Sea Shell City is easy to spot as you're driving down US 1, with its bright blue walls, painted signage, and vibrant ocean murals depicting plunging orcas, snorkelers along the reef, and beachgoers enjoying the shore. Just a couple blocks west of the Lake Worth Lagoon, the marine-themed retail shop offers an array of shells and coral for sale, alongside t-shirts, jewelry, novelty items, and trinkets. Need a wooden pelican, shark jaw, lobster magnet, or gator teeth in a bottle? This is the place.

Sea Shell City was opened by Jerry Merchant in the late 1960s. Its continuous presence is a flashback to the heyday of roadside attractions and souvenirs shops, only this one has managed to stand the test of time. Run by Virginia Merchant for the majority of its 50+ years in business, her sons Daniel and Raymond Gilbert can now be found greeting customers at the register. The brothers exude pride in their family and store history as they happily showcase their products and legacy.

Custom pieces, like shell-edged mirrors, sit half finished alongside bags of shells available for home craft projects. Loyal customers who visited the shop as children now return with their own kids to shop for dried starfish, while visitors pick up mementos and ask for local recommendations and directions.

As you enter the store, the blue tones continue where patrons are greeted with a smile and one-on-one service to select the perfect beachside necessity or gift. Wind chimes and décor pieces hang from the ceiling overhead as you wander among rows of conch shells, sand dollars, and alligator heads. Brightly colored signs featuring cheeky sayings grace the walls, while souvenirs and Florida-centric clothing fill the racks. The small family business has thrived through the decades because the locals and tourists want to keep coming back.

Address 2100 Broadway Avenue, Riviera Beach, FL 33404, +1 (561) 844-2576 | Getting there From I-95: Take exit 76 and drive east on Blue Heron Boulevard. Turn right on Broadway Avenue. Store and parking on the left. | Hours Daily 10am–6pm | Tip Visit Northwood Village to see a collection of public art murals on exterior walls and shipping containers alongside vibrant local eateries and retail shops (Northwood Road, West Palm Beach, www.northwoodvillage.com).

23— Shopping Mall Masterpiece

Heavy metal and loud art in the back lot

Jason Newsted is a Grammy Award winning Rock and Roll Hall of Fame inductee. Former bassist of the heavy metal band Metallica, Newsted found a new creative outlet in the early 2000s. While he continued his music career through various projects, he began exploring visual arts. Graphic and colorful, his artwork has been featured in various gallery shows and sold for top dollar. However, a very little known secret is the large-scale wall mural in the back parking lot of the Tequesta Fashion Mall. Why would this famous rocker and celebrated artist paint the backside of a strip mall in a sleepy South Florida beach town? Because he is good friends with the owner of a popular restaurant located behind those walls, Chef Erik Petterson.

Jason Newsted was born in Michigan in 1963 and raised on a farm. He garnered his musical interest from his family and their records. In 1986, the bassist Cliff Burton of Metallica tragically died when their tour bus crashed in Sweden. Jason entered the lineup of potential replacements, learning every song in their upcoming tour set prior to his audition. He joined the band and played bass until leaving Metallica in 2001. In 2006, he injured his shoulder, leaving him temporarily unable to play. It was during this time that he found art as an alternative creative outlet. His first solo show, "RaWk," debuted at the Cultural Council for Palm Beach County gallery.

The large-scale wall mural is colorful and chaotic, featuring abstract imagery mixed with tribal, animal-like depictions and lettering. Within the art lies another secret, a handful of strokes painted in fluorescent colors that create a new piece when viewed with a black light! The mural is located on the west back side of the building just off the courtyard of the plaza. Also look for a playful monkey and other sporadic doodles scattered along the wall, all signed "JSUN."

Address 150 N US Highway 1, Tequesta, FL 33469 | Getting there From I-95: Take exit 87A and drive east on Indiantown Road for about three miles. Turn left on Alternate A1A North, then left on US Highway 1. Shopping center and parking on the left. | Hours Unrestricted | Tip Pop into EVO Italian Restaurant for family-inspired recipes and to see more of Newsted's artwork along the walls (150 N US Highway 1, Tequesta, www.evoitalian.com).

24 Square Grouper

Bales, bands, bootleggers, and Buffet

Square Grouper Tiki Bar and Castaways Marina is quintessential Jupiter, with its thatch tiki hut, Adirondack chairs, laid-back bar scene, docked boats, and stunning, unobstructed view of the Jupiter Lighthouse. The site has been featured in several music videos, including the happy hour hit, "It's Five o' Clock Somewhere," by Alan Jackson and Jimmy Buffet. It was also a filming location for the popular *Bachelorette* television series. The scenic watering hole showcases the natural beauty of the Loxahatchee River and is a popular meeting place day or night. But even in its past, the Love Street lot that Square Grouper now calls home was at the heart of Jupiter.

In the 1800s, the site was purchased by Gus Miller to accommodate the builders of the lighthouse the bar now overlooks. A hotel and saloon served workers alongside wealthy travelers making their way on the Indian River. The view attracted guests like President Grover Cleveland, who would stay, dine, dance, and regale alongside those traveling by yacht or steamer along the river. The hotel was eventually abandoned, and the space took on new uses. In the early 2000s, "Square Grouper" opened, a nod to the nickname for bales of marijuana discovered along the shoreline. Often thrown from boats and planes by smugglers, these bundles have been found by authorities and locals. In fact, the site has had a front row seat to centuries of illegal activity, from pirates to rum runners to bank robbers.

Patrons of Square Grouper enjoy live music seven days a week by local and national acts. The vibe is in line with the sleepy surf town, boasting no reservations and no stuffy dress code. Guests 21 and over are invited to dance and relax in the warmth of the South Florida environment and take in the view with just under 20 boat slips available dockside.

Address 1111 Love Street, Jupiter, FL 33477, +1 (561) 406-6417, www.squaregrouper.net | **Getting there** From I-95: Take exit 87A and drive east on Indiantown Road for about four miles. Turn left on US Highway 1, turn right on A1A, then left on Clemons Street. Bar and parking on right. | **Hours** Sun–Thu 11am–midnight, Fri & Sat 11–1am | **Tip** Enjoy a morning coffee or post-dinner sundae at Cones and Coffee (997 N Highway A1A Suite B, Jupiter).

25__ Town & Country Feed
Al Capone's Jupiter Farms hideout

Pulling up to Town & Country Feed & Supply, you might not know the long history associated with this parcel of land, from murderous mobsters to the shining stars of Los Angeles. Although Al Capone is better known for his escapades in Broward and Miami-Dade Counties, the notorious mobster had his hands in Palm Beach County as well. Back in the 1920s, Jupiter Farms Road was known as "Italian Farms Road," and it is rumored that Capone secretly owned the property at number 16133.

Alphonse "Al" Capone was one of the most well-known gangsters in American history. The term "Public Enemy Number One" is based on his top spot on the Chicago Crime Commission's first list of those considered to be the most dangerous to the community. Nicknamed "Scarface," Capone's dealings in bootlegging and brothels and his violent acts made him an infamous figure in American society, so much so that his son Al Jr. changed his name after years of trying to overcome the stigma of being a Capone. The property in Jupiter Farms is rumored to have been a hideout for Capone to take a break from Chicago and Miami while overseeing moonshine shipments moving through the Jupiter Inlet. Longtime residents claim to have watched shady characters come and go from the area during the height of Prohibition.

Actor Burt Reynolds later bought the property as his personal ranch and it was here that he filmed for several motion pictures and married Loni Anderson (see ch. 17). The large acreage has since been divided to create a community called Reynolds Ranch.

Today, Town & Country Feed & Supply stands where the cottage that once allegedly hosted criminals and fugitives stood. A family-owned and operated business, they offer products geared towards equestrians, farmers, and pet owners. Their supplies range from hay to fencing materials, with feeds for a variety of livestock, including cows and horses.

Address 16133 Jupiter Farms Road, Jupiter, FL 33478, +1 (561) 746-0433, www.townandcountryfeedandsupplyinc.com | Getting there From I-95: Take exit 87B and drive west on Indiantown Road. Turn left on Jupiter Farms Road. Store and parking are on the right. | Hours Mon–Fri 9am–6pm, Sat 9am–5pm, Sun 10am–5pm | Tip Experience Jupiter Farms on horseback with lessons and trail rides at Desert Rose Ranch (1700 SE Ranch Road, Jupiter, www.desertroseranch-fl.com).

26 Turtle Walk

Explore and observe with Loggerhead Marinelife

While the 12,000-square-foot Loggerhead Marinelife Center in Juno Beach was built in 2007, its history goes back over three decades. A non-profit organization, their focus is education and conservation of marine life, with a special emphasis on sea turtles. The original vision was that of the Center's founder Eleanor Fletcher, a local resident who had noticed the high number of sea turtle nests along the beach's shoreline. Curious about the movements of hatchlings, she began studying sea turtles and the impact of human development on their ecosystem. Earning her nickname, "The Turtle Lady," Fletcher decided to take the approach of educating the next generation as a way of protecting the species. Classes held at her home grew into the Children's Museum of Juno Beach and eventually became The Marinelife Center of Juno Beach.

What is now the Loggerhead Marinelife Center, hosts over 350,000 guests each year and educates 75,000 registered students through exhibits, classes, excursions, and camps. During sea turtle nesting and hatching season, you can go on turtle walks and experience the process. This after-hours tour takes you along the beach to visit sea turtle nests and safely observe females laying eggs or hatchlings making their way to the ocean depending on the time of season. The walks are state-permitted, guided by experienced scouts, and utilize specialized equipment for the safety of the turtles.

The center is open year-round for you to meet sea turtle patients being cared for at the on-site veterinary hospital, and you can explore the exhibit hall too. Ocean conservation programming is available for a more in-depth or educational experience, including talks, guided tours, beach clean-ups, and eco-adventures. Guests are also invited to "adopt" sea turtle patients and monitored nests. If you happen to see "Fletch," their friendly turtle mascot, make sure to give him a high five!

Address 14200 US Highway 1, Juno Beach, FL 33408, +1 (561) 627-8280, www.marinelife.org | Getting there From I-95: Take exit 83 and drive east on Donald Ross Road about four miles. Turn left onto US Highway 1. Center and parking lot are on the right. | Hours Daily 10am–5pm | Tip Just down the road is Manatee Lagoon featuring seasonal manatee viewing, an educational center and marine life exhibits (6000 N Flagler Drive, West Palm Beach, www.visitmanateelagoon.com).

27 Waters of the World

Dip into international waters at PGA National Resort

Home of the Honda Classic golf tournament and infamous Bear Trap three-hole stretch, PGA National offers a full-service resort, five championship courses, and a world-class spa. A popular destination for tourists and residents, the Jack Nicklaus-redesigned Champion Course has built a name for itself, being hailed as one of the most difficult courses in Florida and on the PGA Tour. For those looking for a more relaxing visit, the spa has a pool deck featuring three large pools. But rather than pondering salt vs. chlorine, you should really be asking where in the world the water is from.

Each mineral pool is modeled after a famed body of water. The Dead Sea pool is designed to match the salinity of its namesake located between Jordan and Israel. One of the saltiest bodies of water in the world, the Dead Sea gives you a feeling of floating versus swimming, even though it is notorious for being an unfriendly environment to marine life. The Salies de Béarn pool mimics the waters of the area in southwest France, with salts imported from the French Pyrenees. The salinity is believed to relieve muscle pain, tension, and stress, while toning the skin you lounge in the pool. Bathers seeking heat over salt can soak in the hot tub.

The Spa at PGA National offers a variety of restorative services, from salt glows and mud wraps to facials and peels, and the full salon features hair and nail care. Therapists perform a lengthy menu of massage techniques inspired by treatments across the globe. Choose from soothing Swedish strokes, Hawaiian Lomi Lomi, Japanese Shiatsu, or immersive Watsu bodywork, and then go relax poolside. The Waters of the World Café offers guests a lighter fare of salads and sandwiches with refreshing cocktails, like vodka watermelon coolers, and frosé. Access is included with a minimum spa treatment, and day passes are also available for a fee to enjoy a dip or rent a cabana for the afternoon.

Address 400 Avenue of the Champions, Palm Beach Gardens, FL 33418, +1 (561) 627-1800, www.pgaresort.com | Getting there From I-95: Take exit 79 and drive west on PGA Boulevard. Turn left on Avenue of the Champions. Continue through the roundabout. Resort and parking on the left. | Hours Daily 8:30am – 6pm | Tip Hit the links on the public North Palm Beach Country Club course, also designed by Nicklaus (951 US-1, North Palm Beach, www.village-npb.org).

28 — 1000 Mermaids

Swim in a sea of mermaids

About one mile southeast of Lake Worth Inlet and below the waves is a growing collection of mythical sea creatures made of sustainable concrete. *1000 Mermaids* is a monumental environmental public art initiative aimed at using the human connection to mythical mermaids to lure divers to the ocean floor, bring awareness to reef restoration, and support vital marine habitat.

1000 Mermaids is a non-profit, artificial reef EcoArt project with the goal of placing 1,000 sculptures into the ocean to create a reef. Christopher Xavier O'Hare of Reef Cells has concepted and constructed dynamic reef components designed to encourage colonization of coral growth, create internal corridors for juvenile fish to seek protection from predators, and emulate natural reef aesthetics for both divers and marine life. Mermaids are a welcome departure from the more common use of obsolete ships, trains, and vehicles for this purpose.

In August 2019, the first deployment of 18 modules was successfully completed, and a second followed with dozens more mermaids. Deployments will occur on an annual basis. The sculptures are placed with diver direction and are designed to create a thriving environment for the living coral reef population. A fascinating aspect of this venture is the utilization of patented Coral Lok fasteners. Interlocking plugs and receivers make installation easy and allow for coral fragments to be implanted for natural integration. This innovative technology could change the way corals are outplanted from labs and introduced seamlessly across the globe.

The site is diver-friendly. Look for plaques with quotes and a mermaid tail base to pose in for underwater selfies. Schools of fish move through the structures, which have already begun to see marine life growth. Find more Reef Cell designs at dive sites like Firehock Memorial and Phil Foster Park.

Address N 26°45.2703'; W 080°01.6392', +1 (954) 361-4998, www.1000mermaids.com, info@1000mermaids.com | Getting there The site is accessible by boat, privately or chartered through a diving service | Hours Unrestricted | Tip Don't miss the annual Boynton Beach Haunted Pirate Fest and Mermaid Splash (100 NE 4th Street, Boynton Beach, www.bbpiratefest.com).

29 Aioli on Dixie

First sourdough bakery in West Palm Beach

The Dixie corridor has become a hotspot for local talent to build a brick and mortar around their culinary concepts. Driving through South End, there are hidden gems from some of the best chefs in the area, from Chef Clay Carne's Latin street food at Cholo Soy Cocina to Chef Matthew Byrne's contemporary American at Kitchen. Nestled within the drive is the eatery and bakery Aioli, run by Chef Michael and Melanie Hackman.

Walking through the doors of Aioli, you can see the crew bustling in the background, baking bread and preparing sandwiches. The love child of the Hackmans, Aioli is truly a family run operation. The husband and wife team can be found regularly behind the register, driving a delivery van with one of their daughters in the passenger seat, or working the weekend green market during season. Chef Michael earned his stripes in some of the most respected kitchens of Palm Beach including The Breakers and Café L'Europe. He traveled to San Francisco and staged in well-known bakeries from California to New York, perfecting his sourdough and viennoiserie programs. Opening in 2014, Aioli specializes in chef-driven casual fare that caters to the local community, appealing to a discerning lunch crowd and baked good aficionados alike. Patrons can be seen leaving with their locally beloved everything croissants, sourdough-based sandwiches, and "crack coffee."

Aioli expanded their operations in 2018 with a downtown West Palm Beach location catering to the residents and working crowd surrounding South Olive Avenue. Their breads and pastries can also be found on restaurant menus throughout the area through wholesale partnerships, while the Hackmans and their team are frequently seen at events supporting local causes and fundraising efforts. Breakfast and lunch goers can expect their meal to come with a side of community and conversation.

Roasted Golden Beets
Goat Cheese, Hardboiled Egg, Red Onion, Mixed Greens, Whole Grain Mustard Vinaigrette 10.75

Quiche of the Day
Side Garden Salad 9.50

Soup
Cup 4   Bowl 6
...use, vegetarian & gluten free unless specified otherwise

Tomato, Fresh Mozzarella, Pesto on Ciabatta 10.50

Roasted Vegetable
Goat Cheese, Arugula on Ciabatta 10.50

Long Stem Artichoke & Pesto
Roasted Pepper, Fresh Mozzarella on Ciabatta 10.50

Roast Beef & Caramelized Onion
Cheddar Cheese, Horseradish on Ciabatta 10.75

Turkey & Cheddar
Roasted Tomato Aioli on Ciabatta 10.50

Grilled Three Cheese
Cheddar, Parmesan, Gorgonzola, Brie or Mozzarella, Butter Bread 8.50
add Tomato .50 add Ham 1.00 add Bacon 2.00

Tuna Salad
Cucumber, Lettuce, Tomato on House Made Seven Grain 10.50

Chicken Salad
Lettuce, Tomato, Onion, Walnuts on House Made Seven Grain 10.80

Roast Beef
Horseradish, Tomato, Lettuce, Onion on House Made Seven Grain 10.75

"All Meats are Natural & Sodium Nitrate Free"
Produced in a facility that uses nuts, wheat, soy and milk.

Address 7434 S Dixie Highway, West Palm Beach, FL 33405, +1 (561) 366-7741, www.aioliwpb.com | Getting there From I-95: Take exit 66 and drive east on Forest Hill Boulevard. Turn right on US Highway 1. Restaurant is on the left. | Hours Mon–Sat 7am–4pm | Tip Visit another family affair with the three-brother team behind Celis Produce just down the road offering acai bowls, smoothies, and fresh produce (2814 S Dixie Highway D, West Palm Beach, www.celis-produce.com).

30 Armory Art Center
From farm stand to easel

The Armory Art Center is a comprehensive arts education center that has hosted a myriad of notables, including former First Lady and Senator Hillary Clinton, opera star Luciano Pavarotti, movie stars Burt Reynolds and Loni Anderson, and *Star Trek's* Leonard Nimoy, through their programming of speeches, exhibits, and classes. Set around the geometric, two-story Streamline Moderne building, the campus embraces its armory past. While today the focus is art, this registered historical place has seen its days of produce, pistols, and prom nights.

The Armory building was originally built as a vegetable stand to sell the harvests coming into town from the areas surrounding Lake Okeechobee. With the Great Depression came the New Deal, and during the time of World War II, the Armory was constructed around parts of the original configuration. Soldiers trained on site and repaired military vehicles, while the vault stored various weapons and ammunition. With the end of the war came creative uses for the complex, including social events and entertainment. Eventually, the building was abandoned, as there was no demand for military support. With the closing of the Norton School of Art just down the street in the late 1980s, the structure was once again resurrected, this time by the art community.

The Armory Art Center is made up of three buildings, including the hallmark 1939 Art Deco design by William Manly King. Visitors and students of all ages can experience courses in their state-of-the-art studios and shows in their galleries, plus lectures and special events held throughout the property. The Young Artists Studio is the newest addition and was designed specifically to allow ample natural light for painters. The historic space is still available for private social and corporate engagements, including the lovely Morris & Rose Kraft sculpture gardens.

Address 811 Park Place, West Palm Beach, FL 33401, +1 (561) 832-1776, www.armoryart.org | Getting there From I-95: Take exit 69A and drive east on Belvedere Road. Turn left on Parker Avenue. Turn right onto Park Place. Center and parking on the left. | Hours Mon–Thu 10am–6pm, Fri & Sat 10am–4pm | Tip The Armory Art Center sits at the southern tip of Howard Park which has its own historic past and modern day amenities (1302 Parker Avenue, West Palm Beach, www.wpb.org).

31 The Barefoot Mailman

Buried Palm Beach stories at Woodlawn Cemetery

"That which is so universal as death must be a blessing," greets visitors as they pass under the towering arched entryway at Woodlawn Cemetery. Home to three cemeteries within its gates including the Jewish Cemetery, the 17-acre burial ground was the creation of Henry Flagler (see ch. 39). Situated among pineapple fields, the space was developed in 1904 and soon became an attraction for tourists and locals to visit. The landscape has changed over the years, as banyan trees were removed, gravesites and acreage added, and greenery has matured around the tombs.

Charles Edward Merrill, co-founder of Merrill Lynch, is buried here in the company of E. M. Brelsford, and you'll find the mass grave of 96 victims of the 1928 Okeechobee Hurricane. Joe Sakai, the Japanese-born founder of the Yamato Colony in Boca Raton, rests here, as does Charlie Pierce, one of the original "Barefoot Mailmen," who carried mail to and from Palm Beach in the late 1800s. A term coined in the 1940s, the Barefoot Mailmen were a storied team of mail carriers who were known for their unique route. With limited road access from Palm Beach to Miami, they completed much of their deliveries by boat and walking barefoot on the packed sands of the beach. It took them just under a week to cover over 100 miles round trip.

Walkways allow for a peaceful stroll through the grounds, where statues of angels, crosses, urns, and tombstones can be viewed alongside mausoleums and allow a place of mourning for families. Moonlight Cemetery Tours are available to visit the graveyard and hear the stories of the final resting place of many early pioneers from the region. While Henry Flagler has a gravesite in the center mausoleum, it is empty. Flagler changed his last wishes following a plot by two founders of West Palm Beach to incorporate Palm Beach behind his back. He was interred in St. Augustine with his family.

THAT WHICH IS SO UNIVERSAL AS DEATH
MUST BE A BLESSING

Address 1301 S Dixie Highway, West Palm Beach, FL 33401, www.wpb.org/government/city-clerk/woodlawn-cemetery | **Getting there** From I-95: Take exit 70 and drive east on Okeechobee Boulevard. Turn right on US Highway 1. Cemetery and parking on the right | **Hours** Daily 7am–3:30pm | **Tip** To visit the mass gravesite of almost 700 victims of the 1928 Okeechobee Hurricane, make your way to Pauper's Cemetery, the Hurricane of 1928 African-American Mass Burial Site (Intersection of 25th Street and Tamarind Avenue).

32 Belk's General Store
Gangster poker in the back room

A small convenience store at the heart of its community, Belk's General Store has been around since the 1920s. From allegedly selling bootleg moonshine during Prohibition, to ring fights in the back parking lot, the former post office building has seen its share of exciting times. Serving as a water cooler to the Greenacres area for almost a century, its regulars have often paid via the honor system and IOUs. Their familiarity with one another is strong – a new face often belongs to someone who is lost and asking for directions.

Belk's has a lot of stories to tell – and plenty it will never reveal. It is rumored that John Dillinger, notorious gangster, bank robber, and friend of Al Capone (see ch. 25), frequented the shop and played poker in a backroom. He was gunned down by police outside of a Chicago movie theater in July 1934, just months after one such game. More than 5,000 people visited the cemetery the day of his burial, despite efforts to keep the specifics under wraps. Locals recall nights when he slept on the roof after particularly rowdy poker games. In 1984, the exterior of the store was at the heart of a missing person's case. Eight-year-old Marjorie "Christy" Luna vanished after a quick stop for cat food. Her story reemerged in the 2000s, when the police department took the unorthodox approach of having the missing girl "take over" their Twitter account for the day, retracing her fateful movements from an eerie first person perspective. Though several inventive campaigns have resulted in leads, the case remains cold to this day.

Belk's General Store's name goes back to its first owner Sonny Belk, Sr. Today, Belk's continues to service its surrounding community as a corner store and grocer. Locals know that the side kitchen makes tasty Mexican tortas and tacos, while neighbors from the community catch up with each other at the front of the store.

Address 300 Swain Boulevard, Greenacres, FL 33463, +1 (561) 355-5588 | Getting there
From I-95: Take exit 64 and drive east on 10th Avenue. Turn left on Swain Boulevard.
Belk's General Store will be located on the left. | Hours Mon–Thu 6am–11:30pm, Fri
6:30am–midnight, Sat 7am–midnight, Sun 7am–noon | Tip Visit the Seller's House
and Farm, sometimes called the "Dillinger House," at Yesteryear Village (9067 Southern
Boulevard, West Palm Beach, www.southfloridafair.com).

33 Bethesda-by-the-Sea
The Spanish Memorial

The Church of Bethesda-by-the-Sea is the oldest house of worship in Palm Beach. Built from driftwood and packing boxes, the original 1889 Bethesda-by-the-Sea structure held 100 congregants, who would travel up to three hours each way to attend. The church grew, and the congregation moved up the island to the church's current location in a gothic revival structure. Styled after the 13th-century Leon Cathedral, the interior features *Te Deum* stained-glass windows above the high altar and museum-quality artwork.

The church is steeped in history. Engraved into the cornerstone are the years 1513 and 1925, respectively, the year Juan Ponce de León arrived in Florida and the year the community broke ground on the new church, which welcomed worshippers back the following Christmas. Held within this cornerstone is a letter of support from the Spanish King Alfonso XIII, who took the throne in 1902. The church was meant to be a Spanish memorial, set in what was once considered New Spain, as a "token of Christian unity and international friendship," according to letters written by Alfred James Sheldon of the church.

Notable weddings include that of President Donald Trump and Melania Trump before their star-studded Mar-a-Lago reception in 2005 (see ch. 64). Chicago Bulls star Michael Jordan and Yvette Prieto held their ceremony here in 2013 before over a thousand guests descended upon the Bears Club in Jupiter.

You should go play tourist for the day and book a Diva Duck tour for amazing views of Bethesda-by-the-Sea from the water. Touted as "unsinkable," the bright blue Hydra-Terra duck boat is a Coast Guard-approved vessel that safely transitions from bus to boat. Take in the South Florida fresh air as you float past historical sites, celebrity homes, and much more – with commentary, insights, and musical interludes from experienced guides.

Address 141 S County Road, Palm Beach, FL 33480, +1 (561) 655-4554, www.bbts.org |
Getting there From I-95: Take exit 70 and drive east on Okeechobee Boulevard. Continue
on Okeechobee Boulevard. Drive to S County Road in Palm Beach Way. Turn left onto S
County Road. Location and parking will be on the right. | **Hours** Mon–Fri 9am–5pm, Sat
9am–4pm, Sun 8am–1pm | **Tip** Take a short walk to go pay homage to the beloved Giant
Kapok Tree, a species from the Amazon rainforest with an enormous trunk. It's almost
200 years old (S Lake Trail, Palm Beach).

34 Big Dog Rescue Ranch
Finding forever homes

Big Dog Rescue Ranch is much more than a place to adopt a large canine. It is the largest cage-free, no-kill dog rescue in the US, with a bona fide animal rights activist at the helm. Founded in 2008, the shelter has saved over 40,000 dogs and aspires to saving 5,000 more each year. Offering services from medical care to therapy, animals are guided through the process from rescue through to fostering and adoption.

Lauree Simmons, the president and founder of Big Dog Ranch Rescue, is an award-winning designer and building contractor whose background in custom home design led to the creation of one of the most thoughtfully planned dog rescue facilities in the country. Inspired by a trip to a kill shelter, Simmons returned home with a vehicle full of dogs and a vision for a place that could rehabilitate them to their best mental and physical condition for rehoming. A third generation Palm Beach native, her nurturing influence reaches far beyond the 33 acres that make up the campus.

Big Dog Rescue Ranch has become a haven for animals displaced by natural disasters, providing food, medical supplies, and shelter to those in need. Simmons has personally fought animal abuse through her involvement in getting a bill passed that makes animal cruelty a federal offense for the first time in US history, and her work against kill shelters in the US and dog meat trade abroad in countries like China. She has become a global voice for a population that can't speak for themselves.

Big Dog Rescue Ranch assists in the placement of dogs big and small. Through various programs like "Pets for Patriots" and "Seniors for Seniors," the organization is able to pair pets of all breeds and ages with forever loved ones. Local residents are invited to apply to become a volunteer, foster or adopt, or donate to the cause. Or show your support by shopping at the retail store.

Address 14444 Okeechobee Boulevard, Loxahatchee Groves, FL 33470, +1 (561) 791-6465, www.bdrr.org, info@bdrr.org | **Getting there** From I-95: Take exit 70 and drive west on Okeechobee Boulevard for about 12 miles. Ranch and parking are on the left. | **Hours** Daily 10am–5pm | **Tip** Animal lovers may enjoy a visit to Peggy Adams Rescue League (3200 N Military Trail, Unit 3100, West Palm Beach, www.peggyadams.org).

35 Bike the Lake Trail

Shirts not required

Palm Beach Lake Trail is a pedestrian and cycling trail that winds along the Lake Worth Lagoon for approximately six miles up the west side of the island. Set between the backside of private property lines and their docks, this paved trail provides an insider glimpse into the island's estates. Wandering along the trail, visitors are able to view spectacular Palm Beach homes, custom dock gates, the waterway, and classic island landmarks. The trail is often active on mild weather days with families cycling, walking, and jogging along the long walls of vines and bougainvillea.

The Lake Trail was the focal point of a promiscuous battle on the island when Allen DeWeese, a public defender, began jogging the trail bare-chested and was subsequently arrested. What ensued was a seven-year-long battle in the courts that ended with the Town Council finally dropping the charges and offending ordinances in 1986. The argument was one of principle. DeWeese took the side of civil liberties against the council, which rested on the side of maintaining decorum and conforming to a certain level of proper dress within the elite community. In the end, federal courts found the council to be simply meddling in the fashion choices of its public beyond their authority.

The trail is free to use and motorist-free, with few interruptions, and wayfinding signs keep you on the course. Points of interest along the trail include Flagler Museum (see ch. 73), Seagull Cottage, Society of the Four Arts (see ch. 84), Duck's Nest, and Sailfish Club just before its northern tip at the Inlet Dock. Keep an eye out for statues and plaques commemorating those who influenced the area, like E. R. Bradley and Elisha Newton Dimick. For a longer trip, you can easily extend your ride into the island down County Road or across the eastern side along Ocean Boulevard. As ever, bring your sunscreen and water.

Address Lake Trail, Palm Beach, FL 33480 | **Getting there** From I-95: Take exit 70 and drive east on Okeechobee Boulevard. Continue straight onto Royal Park Bridge which turns into Royal Palm Way. Look for metered parking along the west side of the island for access to the trail. | **Hours** Daily dawn–dusk | **Tip** Visit the Palm Beach Bicycle Trail Shop for a trail map, bike rentals or sales, and repairs (50 Cocoanut Row, Suite 117, Palm Beach, www.palmbeachbicycle.com).

36 Brazilian Court

The allure of yesterday meets the comfort of today

The second-oldest hotel on the island, The Brazilian Court is a 1926 Spanish Colonial style that exudes Old Palm Beach charm. It is also home to the renowned Café Boulud, headed by James Beard Award winner and Michelin star chef Daniel Boulud. Originally designed by Rosario Candela the hotel saw a facelift in the 1930s by famed architect Maurice Fatio.

Brazilian Court has seen renovations over the years with a common thread, adding the comforts of today to the comforts of yesterday. Centered by two courtyards, the property became a favorite for the rich and famous to stay and enjoy their outdoor privacy before entering the social scene. The hotel's signature pale lemon yellow façade and barrel tile roof allow the crisp white trim and green palms of the fabled courtyards to pop.

Decades of lounging movie stars, mingling socialites, celebrity weddings, and food and wine festivals have graced the furnishings and surrounded the centerpiece fountain. The hotel has seen the glitz as well as the gloom of famous names. David Kennedy, son of Robert F. Kennedy, died of an overdose in Room 107 in 1984, though the rooms have since been re-numbered. Business magnates, distinguished actors and affluent travelers can be seen dining on the terrace overlooking the main courtyard or sipping cocktails inside at the dramatic backlit marble bar of Café Boulud.

Nestled between Brazilian and Australian just blocks from Worth Avenue and the beach, the historic landmark features a pristine location for 80 guest rooms and suites. The award-winning property is infused with the glamour of the 1920s, boasting luxurious fabrics, meticulous woodwork, and a sophisticated color palette. Guests are greeted by the La Passage lounge and check-in before making their way into hallways of rich mahogany wood and jewel-toned furnishings en route to their timelessly plush accommodations.

Address 301 Australian Avenue, Palm Beach, FL 33480, +1 (561) 655-7740, www.thebraziliancourt.com | **Getting there** From I-95: Take exit 70 and drive east on Okeechobee Boulevard about three miles. Cross the bridge over the Intracoastal Waterway onto Royal Palm Way. Turn right onto S Lake Drive, then left on Australian Avenue. Hotel is on the left. Valet parking and street parking available. | **Hours** Open daily | **Tip** Visit Palm Beach Grill for dinner. Previously called Au Bar, this is the space where the 1991 scandal involving John F. Kennedy's nephew, William Kennedy Smith, began (340 Royal Poinciana Way, Palm Beach, www.palmbeachgrill.com).

37 — Buccan's Chef Conley

Small plates and big flavors

One of the most celebrated restaurants on the island, Buccan is the handiwork of Chef Clay Conley and his partners. Opened in 2011, the modern and refined yet casual lounge and dining room are credited with transforming the area's food scene. The menu is focused around small plates and features an eclectic mix of elevated takes on familiar comfort foods, like the Hot Dog Panini, alongside handmade pasta with seasonal truffle, and wood-fired local fish. Come here to unwind in the lounge's couches and armchairs beside the lively bar area. This is a place to see and be seen, with the added benefit of experiencing flavors and dishes from around the world.

Clay Conley was born in Maine and trained under Todd English in Boston. But he became a breakout star in Miami as the executive chef of Mandarin Oriental. Nominated for *Best Chef: South* by the James Beard Foundation five times, his talents have been recognized far beyond county lines. A proponent of No Kid Hungry, Conley sits as a Chef Chair for the annual Palm Beach's Taste of the Nation and hosts one of the most lucrative No Kid Hungry fundraising dinners in the country. Conley is a fixture at the Palm Beach Food and Wine Festival, kicking off every year with his "First Bite" dinner. And he has earned his place as one of the top chefs in South Florida. From his childhood on a farm to his international adventures, his creativity and passion are expressed through balanced and inspired plates using seasonal ingredients.

The Buccan team has expanded with the Sandwich Shop, connected sister restaurant Imoto serving sushi and Asian fare, an Italian venture Grato in the nearby Dixie Corridor, and most recently, Chateau Miami in Brickell and philanthropic non-profit Buccan Provisions. All of the restaurants in their portfolio create sophisticated yet approachable foods, design, and atmosphere.

Address 350 S County Road, Palm Beach, FL 33480, +1 (561) 833-3450, www.buccanpalmbeach.com, info@buccanpalmbeach.com | Getting there From I-95: Take exit 70 and drive east on Okeechobee Boulevard. Cross the bridge onto Royal Palm Way. Turn right on S County Road. Restaurant is on the right. | Hours Daily 5–10pm | Tip Enjoy Southern-inspired cuisine by fellow James Beard Award nominee and *Top Chef* alumnus Lindsay Autry at The Regional Kitchen and Public House (651 Okeechobee Boulevard, West Palm Beach, www.eatregional.com).

38 Bulk Candy Store
Sweets by the handful

The name on the door is pretty self-explanatory, and the Bulk Candy Store is just that. Featuring hundreds of varieties of candies, dozens of flavored popcorns, chocolates, chewing gums, sodas, and sweets, their selection is vast and vibrant. You can pick from a wall of PEZ dispensers, enjoy nostalgic bites like a Charleston Chew or Bit-O-Honey, and experience candy bars from around the world, such as the Cadbury collection from England. Outside of the candy wrapper-esque purple and yellow building, their mobile popup is better known as the "World's Largest Travelling Candy Store."

The Bulk Candy Store is a family owned and operated business, and each member wears a different hat. For Brian Shenkman, one of those duties is the traveling, 2,000-square-foot candy store that graces the fairgrounds of counties from Texas up the East Coast through Florida and the Carolinas and north to Ohio. In each city, fairgoers can enjoy rows of bulk candies and slush beverages, deep fried candy bars, sandwiches, and cookies. The offerings change with each location, depending on the available space and the particular tastes of the area's population, whether that's fruity and spicy or creamy and chewy. The sweet and colorful attraction is a popular stop for children and adults every January at their hometown South Florida Fair.

You are invited to shop at the retail store for your own enjoyment, or attend the large-scale events with "by the pound" and individually packaged goods. Brides are seen leaving with bags to build their own receptions' candy buffets, while expectant mothers stock up on jars of pinks or blues for baby showers. If you want a closer look and taste of the shop, don't miss the Evolution of Candy Tour, usually led by Ken Shenkman. In under an hour, Ken covers everything from the history of candy and how nostalgic treats are made, to taste testing beloved treats.

Address 235 N Jog Road, West Palm Beach, FL 33413, +1 (561) 540-1600, www.bulkcandystore.com | **Getting there** From I-95: Take exit 68 and drive west on Southern Boulevard. Turn right on N Jog Road, then left on Wallis Road. Store and parking located on the left. | **Hours** Mon–Fri 9am–5pm, Sat 10am–2pm | **Tip** Visit Bee Unique for honey-based naturally sweet treats and wax goods (3311 S Dixie Highway, West Palm Beach, www.worldsfinestrawhoney.com).

39__Censored at The Breakers

Scantily clad feminism takes flight on the island

One of the most iconic properties of Palm Beach, The Breakers (originally The Palm Beach Inn) was built by Henry Flagler in the late 1890s (see ch. 31). Just after the turn of the century, the hotel experienced its first fire, and its second in 1925 that left much of the property destroyed. One of the survivors of the 1925 fire was none other than Titanic survivor Margaret Tobin Brown, also known as "Unsinkable Molly Brown." Each time the hotel was rebuilt, it came back bigger and grander than before. In 1926, it reopened with the flair of Shultze and Weaver, a nod to Villa Medici in Rome, and an expansive lobby greeting guests at arrival. The Breakers became a stomping ground for Rockefellers, Vanderbilts, US Presidents, and European royalty alike.

In the 1920s, Evangeline Johnson, daughter of Robert Wood Johnson of Johnson & Johnson, shook up the sunny scene by breaking the censorship rule in a revealing swimsuit. Notorious for their strict guidelines, beach censors would literally measure the length of swimwear to ensure that it was appropriate and that the color was dark enough to not be confused with bare skin. Women might choose to remain clothed at the beach to avoid being berated by censors yelling, "Ladies! Rules is rules!"

During her campaign against the city for women's rights, Johnson piloted a private plane and dropped printed flyers down the beach in support of her cause. The "One-Woman War" against Palm Beach was even featured in her 1990 obituary.

Today, The Breakers is a stunning 140-acre property featuring a luxury resort with oceanfront guest suites, the oldest golf course in Florida, and a world-class spa. The halls glisten during the holiday season, while banquets hosts a portfolio of galas and events throughout the year. It is a sought-after venue for weddings, including those of Sofia Vergara, Nick Swisher, and Rush Limbaugh.

Address 1 S County Road, Palm Beach, FL 33480, +1 (561) 655-6611, www.thebreakers.com |
Getting there From I-95: Take exit 70 and drive east on Okeechobee Boulevard about three
miles. Cross the bridge over the Intracoastal Waterway onto Royal Palm Way. Turn left on
S County Road, right on Breakers Row to The Breakers. Valet parking available. | **Hours** Open
daily | **Tip** Shop for a new swimsuit and resort wear at C. Orrico (336 S County Road, Palm
Beach, www.corrico.com).

40 Church Mouse Thrifting

Where one socialite's trash is another's treasure

Just steps from Worth Avenue, this 4,500 square foot thrift shop has been recognized as one of the top donation-based resale shops in the country. Truly an example of "one's trash is another's treasure," Church Mouse is an excellent opportunity to purchase luxury pieces at an affordable price. Offering gently used high-end designer clothing, handbags, accessories, furniture, crystal, and home goods, the boutique is heavily run by volunteers and benefits The Church of Bethesda-by-the-Sea (see ch. 33).

Shoppers frequently find deals on Chanel, Louis Vuitton, Hermes, Christian Louboutin, and other name brands and designers. Famous island frequenters, like Martha Stewart, can be seen browsing the carefully curated stock, alongside local society figures. A collector's dream, vintage books and toys are commonly found to have surprising value when appraised, and many use the shop as an opportunity to upcycle high-quality goods for their own designer vision. A signifier to the expectant shoppers that season has begun, opening day is typically marked by a line down the street just prior to the October opening of the doors. "The Mouse" runs through season and closes as summer approaches with their famous end-of-season sale in June.

Due to its popularity, Church Mouse's shoppers become regulars in order to get at the ever-changing inventory. You'll never feel "buyer's remorse" over your purchases because of the discounted prices, and the proceeds support a good cause. Whether you're maintaining a rotating closet or purchasing your first Gucci, The Church Mouse has treasures for everyone. The store has been in business for five decades and has donated over $10 million to various charities, supporting outreach, education, food pantries, and shelters in the community. And while their front doors remain closed for the summer months, donations are accepted year-round.

Address 378 S County Road, Palm Beach, FL 33480, +1 (561) 659-2154, www.bbts.org/about-us/church-mouse | Getting there From I-95: Take exit 70 and drive east on Okeechobee Boulevard about three miles. Cross the bridge over the Intracoastal Waterway onto Royal Palm Way. Turn right onto S County Road. Store is on the right with a parking lot behind the building. | Hours Mon–Sat 10am–4pm | Tip Travel north up County Road and visit the island Goodwill boutique for more thrifty luxury finds (210 Sunset Avenue, Palm Beach, www.gulfstreamgoodwill.org).

41 Coral Sky Amphitheatre

A colorful display on and off the stage at sunset

While the name may have changed over the past couple decades, the outdoor music venue that sits just west of the turnpike will forever be known by locals as "Coral Sky." Named for the vivid colored sunsets that illuminate the lawn of concertgoers, this open-air venue has been the epicenter of musical acts coming to Palm Beach County. With seating for just under 20,000, the stage features rows of covered reserved seats while the "lawn" opens up to a grassy, stadium-style general admission area that fills with blankets and eager fans as showtime nears.

Since 1996, ticket holders have searched for seats at Mars Music, Sound Advice, Cruzan, Perfect Vodka, and iThink Financial Amphitheatre as sponsors have come and gone, making Coral Sky the most name-changed amphitheatre in the United States. Some of the biggest tours in the country have graced the Coral Sky stage, which has hosted festivals like OzzFest, Lilith Fair, and season-long passes, like the Country Megaticket, featuring headliners Luke Bryan and Rascal Flatts.

In 1998, Coral Sky was the kick off performance of the US leg of the Spice Girls' Spiceworld Tour, and Dave Matthews has played here over three dozen times with two-night summer shows. The spacious property accommodates multi-stage events, like Warped Tour, plus VIP venues, and an array of concessions and merchandise tents. Regardless of the talent, the breathtaking sunsets have solidified this venue's nickname in shades of orange, pink, and purple.

The key to any Coral Sky experience is the pre-show tailgate. Hundreds of cars fill the surrounding parking lots stocked with coolers, cornhole boards, and enthusiastic fans reminiscent of a rivalry football game. Neighboring vehicles bond over musical tastes and competitive yard games.

Bring sunscreen and pace yourself while the party continues on the lawn as the sun sets and paints the sky.

Address 601-7 Sansburys Way, West Palm Beach, FL 33411, +1 (561) 795-8883, www.livenation.com | **Getting there** From I-95: Take exit 68 and drive west on Southern Boulevard for about five miles. Turn right on Sansbury Way. Follow signage for parking on the left. | **Hours** See website for schedule | **Tip** For a more intimate concert experience, visit the Mizner Park Amphitheater in Boca Raton, which hosts smaller concerts welcoming approximately 4,000 guests (590 Plaza Real, Boca Raton, www.myboca.us/826/Mizner-Park-Amphitheater).

42 Cracker Johnson House
The Sugar Hill of West Palm

During the early 1900s, the Black Americans experienced the culturally rich movement of the Harlem Renaissance, and James Jerome "Cracker" Johnson, a famed bootlegger and numbers runner, emerged as the "Robin Hood" of the Black community in West Palm Beach. An entrepreneur and philanthropist, he helped bridge the gap during segregation and even loaned the City of West Palm Beach $50,000 to balance the budget during a difficult economic time. His home has since been considered the Sugar Hill of the area.

Born in 1877, the son of a formerly enslaved mother and a white father, Jerome was bestowed the derogatory nickname, "Cracker." Though he was not well educated and lacked the abilities to read and write, he managed to build a diverse portfolio of real estate and businesses, both legitimate and illegal. His influence in the community due to his employment of locals, charitable contributions, and involvement in development gave him an unprecedented seat at the table for a Black man.

He strived to empower and elevate the Black population, while serving as a philanthropist to those around him. Johnson was murdered in 1946 while breaking up a fight in front of his Florida Bar on Rosemary Avenue. It is believed he was actually shot by a hired hitman at the hands of the white mobsters who looked to take over his territory – and his profits.

Johnson built his home in 1926 in what was then the affluent black neighborhood of Freshwater. Mrs. Johnson is remembered by locals for offering young Black men a dip in the coin jar if they dressed for and attended church on Sundays. Since Johnson's passing, the house changed hands and fell into disrepair. Most recently, the property was purchased by real estate investor Todd Durand, who partnered with ex-combat veteran Robert Brooks to restore the historic, two-story house and create a five bedroom home for at-risk military veterans.

Address 719 14th Street, West Palm Beach, FL 33401, +1 (561) 355-5588 | Getting there From I-95: Take exit 74 and drive east on 45th Street. Turn right onto N Australian Avenue, then left onto 15th Street. Turn right onto North Sapodilla Avenue, then right at the first cross street onto 14th Street. House is on the right. | Hours Unrestricted from the outside only | Tip Visit the grave of Cracker Johnson and some of the area's most influential Black citizens at Evergreen Cemetery (2825 Rosemary Avenue, West Palm Beach, www.pbchistoryonline.org).

43 Dade County Bank

Older than its Palm Beach County address

The oldest commercial structure in Palm Beach County actually began its life in Dade County. In 1893, Dade County extended north into the territory of Stuart, now part of Palm Beach and Martin counties. A compact 584 square feet, this octagonal building has seen over a century of development and business. Initially the first savings institution in the region, the property eventually housed a barbershop, dentist office, real estate firm, and beauty shop. In the 1930s, it became "Johnny's Playland," a novelty and trick shop owned by John Eggert that spanned four decades.

Since the 1980s, it has housed the Alumni Association's Palm Beach High School Museum, which was replaced by the Dreyfoos School of the Arts in the 1970s. Inside, the museum's memorabilia includes report cards, yearbooks, and trophies from classes and alumni, including actors Burt Reynolds, George Hamilton, the Rice brothers, and Stephen C. O'Connell, whose name graces the University of Florida's arena.

Even the location of this historic building has been diverse. The story goes that the structure was originally perched on Jupiter Island before being floated down to Palm Beach. After a stint at the corner of Clematis and Olive in the late 1890s, it was relocated to the downtown waterfront, before being donated to the City and moved to its current home. Discussions continue to determine if it will see yet another a new home in Yesteryear Village (see ch. 78).

At its current location within Flagler Park, its surrounding area is enjoyable to explore. Just outside the front door is a massive sculpture that reads "BE ART," meant to be interactive with visitors climbing into the letters for selfies and photographs. The quaint, one-story, wood frame with a cone roof backs up to the 21-story Northbridge Center, known as the "Darth Vader Building" for its reflective black glass and towering presence.

Address 401 N Flagler Drive, West Palm Beach, FL 33401, www.pbhs67.org | **Getting there** From I-95: Take exit 71 and drive east on Palm Beach Lakes Boulevard. Turn right on N Flagler Drive. Building located on the right. Street parking available. | **Hours** By appointment | **Tip** Grab a pint, burger, or pierogi at The Butcher Shop Beer Garden housed in a historic airplane hangar (209 6th Street, West Palm Beach).

44 El Solano House

A stone's throw from Billionaire's Row

The El Solano House sits nestled among the estates of Palm Beach and at the constant eye of many island storms. Designed by Addison Mizner (see ch. 50), El Solano's checkered history begins with a wall.

An addition built by Harold Vanderbilt in the 1920s was deemed too close to the home of Standard Oil heiress Elizabeth Kay. Kay responded by building a wall so high that it cast a shadow on Vanderbilt's property and affected his emotional state. Eventually, Vanderbilt moved and sold the addition to Kay, who built a bridge connecting it to her main house property.

Edward and Evelyn McLean of *Washington Post* and Hope Diamond fame soon became the new owners of El Solano. The curse of the Hope Diamond followed them there, as they unwittingly leased the property to Larry Flynt, who brought with him the firestorm of *Hustler Magazine*. Burying his reputation under the name "E. F. Real Estate," he rented the home and used its stunning landscape as a backdrop for his controversial *Hustler* imagery and as a place for models to tan nude in preparation for photo shoots. As word got out in Palm Beach, *Hustler* was removed from newsstands, and island politicians called for Flynt's exit. John Lennon and Yoko Ono were the next high-profile owners, and they took over the property. But they had barely moved in before Lennon was tragically killed in 1980.

El Solano is just over a mile from Billionaire's Row, a collection of sprawling estates valued in the tens and hundreds of millions of dollars and marked by lots running acres to private beaches and stunning entrances leading to towering mansions. The current record is just over $105 million for La Reverie at 1415 South Ocean Boulevard. Its sale eclipsed the previous record set just six months earlier in the summer of 2019 for late Broadway producer Terry Allen Kramer's La Follia estate with its 210 feet of coastline.

Address 720 S Ocean Boulevard, Palm Beach, FL 33480 | **Getting there** From I-95: Take exit 70 and drive east on Okeechobee Boulevard. Continue straight onto Royal Park Bridge which turns into Royal Palm Way. Turn right onto S County Road. The home is on the right. | **Hours** Unrestricted from the outside only | **Tip** Drive by the late David Koch's El Sarmiento estate, which won the Preservation Foundation's Ballinger award in 2008 (150 S Ocean Boulevard, Palm Beach).

45 FITTEAM Ballpark

A different kind of presidential race

Palm Beach County is home to Major League Baseball spring training for the Washington Nationals, Houston Astros, St. Louis Cardinals, and Miami Marlins. With the opening of the 7,500-seat FITTEAM Ballpark of the Palm Beaches came an elevated spring ballgame experience fit for the big leagues. Offering Craft Corner with over 30 craft beers on tap, local food trucks, party decks, and premium suites this facility also became home to three of the famous racing presidents.

The Washington Nationals are known for their oversized presidential mascots racing during the fourth inning of home games at Nationals Park. Since 2006, the four Mount Rushmore presidents have raced in their corresponding term jerseys, "George" in #1, "Abe" in #16. The towering costumes reach as high as 10 feet tall, which makes for an interesting race. The looks were created by Randy Carfagno Productions of New York and fashioned after a costume he designed for a Bette Midler performance. The visiting presidents were retired from the big stage in 2017 and moved to Florida. Calvin "Cal" Coolidge and Herbert "Herbie" Hover, originally sponsored by the White House Historical Association, and William "Bill" Taft now round the bases in West Palm Beach.

The Ballpark of the Palm Beaches facilities made way for four teams to spring train in the area, the most hosted in one county in the state. In 2019, the Nationals and Astros competed against each other in the World Series, drawing the attention of locals to the talent practicing just down the road. Baseball fans attending a game can choose from a variety of seating locations and price points, including sunny spots on the outfield berm. Hot tickets include sell-out matchups, like when the New York Yankees come to town. The 160-acre ballpark hosts a myriad of events across its eight baseball fields, five multi-sports fields, and the main stadium.

Address 5444 Haverhill Road, West Palm Beach, FL 33407, +1 (561) 500-4487, www.fitteamballpark.com, info@fitteamballpark.com | Getting there From I-95: Take exit 74 and drive west on 45th Street. Turn left on Haverhill Road. Ballpark on left, follow signage for parking. | Hours See website for game schedule | Tip Check for spring training game times for the St. Louis Cardinals and Miami Marlins at Roger Dean Stadium (4751 Main Street, Jupiter, www.rogerdeanchevroletstadium.com).

46 __ Fortune Cookie

An Asian market for chefs in the know

The bustling Fortune Cookie Oriental Supermarket sells a variety of Taiwanese, Japanese, Korean, and Thai goods. Shoppers can find fresh seafood, aisles of Asian ingredients and wares, and a bubble tea stand. The owner, Geoffrey Yao, has been known to secure special request items from New York, offering major city quality selections in his smaller city market. Local chefs have been known to host underground pop ups at the market, with limited-time menus of bao buns and other Asian fare.

Fortune Cookie Oriental Supermarket may not wow you at first glance, with its unassuming, free-standing building filled with shelves and refrigerators of culinary goods. But upon further inspection of packaging and produce, and talking with chefs around town, this shop is a diamond in the rough. The Fortune Cookie has become a destination for a range of shoppers from the serious restaurant chef, to the tinkering home cook, to the curious snacker. Within the aisles is an array of hard-to-find ingredients, sauces, and other products. Local chefs frequent the market to experiment with authentic Asian ingredients, often swapping insight and ideas while they peruse the shelves. Adventurous foodies scan unique flavors of international Oreos, Cheetos, and Lays potato chips. Casual patrons may discover matcha flavored candies, mochi ice creams, and Hello Kitty marshmallows, while connoisseurs can check out with umami salt, shoyu, and bonito flakes.

Fortune Cookie has stood as an Asian market for over four decades. Now family owned and operated, it is a local resource for the Asian community and beyond. Fans of pop culture will be pleased to find that the market offers a variety of food items found throughout and created in Japanese and Korean television shows, anime cartoons, and Manga comics. The most popular of these items are Pocky sticks, Kewpie mayonnaise, and Ramune soda.

Address 2700 Forest Hill Boulevard, West Palm Beach, FL 33406, +1 (561) 433-5818, https://fortunecookiesupermarket.business.site | Getting there From I-95: Take exit 66 and drive west on Forest Hill Boulevard. Make a U-turn at Prairie Road. Market and parking on the right. | Hours Mon–Sat 9am–5pm, Sun 10am–2pm | Tip For a southern option for oriental goods try the aisles of Asian Market (5891 S Military Trail, Lake Worth).

47 Gatorland No More

Watch your toes

A glimpse into the old ways of South Florida, the abandoned Everglades Gatorland stands just outside of the Northeast corner of the Everglades National Park. Originally a gas station run by the former mayor of South Bay, J. C. Bowen, and his wife Mary Lou, Everglades Gatorland opened in 1959 in response to visitors' constantly asking where they could see wildlife in person. The business model was simple: the alligators were caught in the lake behind the building on Highway 27, just south of Belle Glade and South Bay, and put on display. They added a gift shop, and over time, they were able to add more animals to the exhibits, like an exotic ocelot, coati, and a king vulture.

As alligator poaching became problematic in the 1960s, the American alligator was put on the endangered species list in 1967. It was eventually removed in 1987 after the alligator population recovered dramatically in one of the greatest success stories of conservation in US history. However, during this time many roadside zoos were forced out of business due to new regulations on hunting and the care of captive animals. Everglades Gatorland survived the downturn and maintained steady business through the 1980s but began to suffer with the less traffic on US27 as the tourists preferred I-95 and the Florida Turnpike and large scale tourist attractions opened elsewhere in the state. Eventually, the station was closed and deserted. It became a relic of the past.

Today, the original shell of the building stands, overgrown with nature but still emblazoned with a sign that reads, "Live Alligators – Finest Collection of Everglades Animals." The structure has been gutted and deteriorated substantially over the years, but it still gives a snapshot into a tradition of roadside attractions in old South Florida. Just be careful when you visit – the live main attractions were caught very close by.

Address 180-212 US Highway 27, South Bay, FL 33493 | **Getting there** From I-95: Take exit 68 and drive west Southern Boulevard for about 30 miles. Continue on US-98. Turn left on FL-80W. Turn left onto 1st Avenue. Building is on the right. | **Hours** Unrestricted | **Tip** Explore the surrounding area by car to see the vast fields of sugar cane, a major crop of South Florida (www.floridacrystals.com).

48 Ghosts in the Coral Cut
Pretty by day, haunted by night

Traveling along the island's Country Club Road is a serene but eerie stretch known as Coral Cut. For years, stories have emerged from the "Witch's Wall" and the history behind the small, barred window few notice as they pass. Haunting sounds, an inexplicable glow, and harrowing tales have emerged from these rocks, maybe from the ghost of a fatal car crash, souls of kidnapped children trapped in a witch's castle, or past prisoners of a secret dungeon – depending on the storyteller. Suffice it to say, the cut joins a handful of notoriously haunted sites on the pristine island – beautiful by day but harrowing by night.

Many believe the souls that stay within the cut are those of a man who was returning home with his family to visit his mother for Thanksgiving, when he crashed into the curve in the night. Others believe it is the mother of a wealthy Palm Beacher who kept her locked behind the gated window. A popular tale, which gave the wall its nickname, is that of a witch, who would kidnap children and lock them in the dungeon. If someone were to touch the bars, their soul would escape, and then the witch would begin her search for their replacement. The witch theme returns in a variation of the story where she herself was kept in a dungeon and tried to dig her way out of the cut, creating the empty space that now requires bars to keep anyone from escaping.

According to officials however, the site is actually home to a water pump, hence the humming sounds and need for gated entry. During the day, the cut is visually stunning, with 200-foot-high towering walls of coral that have been carved to create a 600-foot-long cut-through, green vegetation billowing over the edge from above. A rare scene along the flat land of South Florida, the cut is a popular bike ride route and photo-friendly stop for engagements, portraits, and baby announcements. Just not at night.

Address 300-326 Country Club Road, Palm Beach, FL 33480 | Getting there From I-95:
Take exit 71 and drive east on Palm Beach Lakes Boulevard. Turn right on US Highway 1,
then left on N Quadrille Avenue, and cross the Flagler Memorial Bridge. Turn left on
Bradley Place. Continue on N Lake Way, then left on Country Club Road. | Hours
Unrestricted | Tip There are also ghost stories along Worth Avenue, at the Cartier Building,
Via Mizner, and Taboo Restaurant (Worth Avenue, www.worth-avenue.com).

49 _ Giraffe Painting

Art is a tall order at Lion Country Safari

You don't have to travel to the Serengeti to experience the wonder of a ride through the wild. Opened in 1967, Lion Country Safari was the country's first drive-through safari park, modeled as a "cageless zoo."

Visitors are invited to drive through the 1,000-animal preserve or travel on foot through SafariWorld. The original preserve design was so immersive that the park was forced to install fences when visitors ignored warnings to not open their doors when approached by more dangerous species like the African lion. Consistently ranked on top zoo lists across the country, the park has been featured in various written works and was the inspiration behind a family theme park adventure during the second season of *The Simpsons* in the episode, "Old Money."

One of the VIP experiences available to guests is an interactive visit with the giraffes. Using her mouth to hold the paintbrush, the giraffe creates bright, 3-color artwork on a 16 x 20 canvas. Participants are able to feed the giraffe, take photos, and watch her create the live painting they'll take home as a momento. A portion of the fee is donated to giraffe conservation efforts. Conservation is a major driving force behind the park, which has developed partnerships to protect animals and the environment on a local and global level. The venue also hosts a range of educational opportunities for young people and adults, including tours and outreach programs.

Lion Country Safari sits on hundreds of acres between the two major zoo exhibits. The drive-through attraction is divided into seven sections, from the Las Pampas grasslands to the Kalahari Bushveldt Plateau. Guests are treated to the majestic African lion in The Gorongosa Reserve and the white rhinoceros in Hwange National Park. The walk-through SafariWorld also offers rides and a 4,000-square-foot water park with over 20 interactive water features.

Address 2003 Lion Country Safari Road, Loxahatchee, FL 33470, +1 (561) 793-1084, www.lioncountrysafari.com | Getting there From I-95: Take exit 68 and drive west on Southern Boulevard for about 11 miles. Turn right on Lion Country Safari Road. | Hours Daily 9:30am–4:30pm | Tip Continue painting and socializing at Uptown Art (510 Evernia Street, West Palm Beach, www.uptownart.com).

50 _ Grave of Johnnie Brown
No more monkey business

In the serene courtyard of Via Mizner rest the only two marked graves on the island of Palm Beach. One of those graves belongs to Johnnie Brown, the beloved spider monkey of famed architect Addison Cairns Mizner (see ch. 84). The tombstone reads, *Johnnie Brown, The Human Monkey, Died April 30, 1927.* Nearby is the grave of "Our Laddie," the pet Scottish Terrier of Rose and Morton Sachs, who lived in Mizner's home after his death.

Johnnie Brown became locally famous in the 1920s as he made his way around Palm Beach on the shoulder of Addison Mizner. Considered a visionary, Mizner had a lasting impact on Palm Beach County architecture, especially in the Boca Raton area. He created Via Mizner between Worth Avenue and Peruvian Avenue after completing the exclusive Everglades Club just across the street (see ch. 60). His designs were primarily Mediterranean and Spanish Colonial Revival, with barrel tile roofs, arched entries, colorful tiles, and wrought iron railings. Via Mizner was inspired by European communities nestled within castle barriers with white stucco walls and climbing bougainvillea. Villa Mizner, Mizner's 1924 five-story home, was located at 1 Via Mizner, which now overlooks the final resting place of Johnnie Brown.

Johnnie Brown led an eventful life from his shoulder perch, in his hand-stitched, silk-lined sombrero. He feuded with silent film actress Marie Dressler, received votes during his unsuccessful 1928 run for mayor of Palm Beach, and was invited to attend *The State of Tennessee v. John Thomas Scopes* trial, also known as the Scopes Monkey Trial, but declined. He was outlived by his owner by only six short years, as Mizner passed away in 1933. There have since been stories of children seeing the ghost of Mizner with his pet monkey in the courtyard, and shopkeepers have been known to leave out a banana or two for Johnnie Brown's ghost.

Address Via Mizner, Worth Avenue, Palm Beach, FL 33480 | **Getting there** From I-95: Take exit 70 and drive east on Okeechobee Boulevard about three miles. Cross the bridge over the Intracoastal Waterway onto Royal Palm Way. Turn right onto Hibiscus Avenue. Turn right onto Worth Avenue. Via Mizner is on the right. Street parking is available. | **Hours** Unrestricted | **Tip** Enjoy lunch under one of the blue umbrella patio tables of Pizza al Fresco (14 Via Mizer, Palm Beach, www.pizzaalfresco.com).

51 — Green's Pharmacy
Laughter is the best medicine

Pick up aspirin where John F. Kennedy snuck away from the crowds and Frank Sinatra enjoyed the chance to chat up the locals. Since 1938, Green's Pharmacy has been filling prescriptions and serving up milkshakes and burgers to the people of the island. Celebrities of the past and present have graced the 82 seats of this classic luncheonette nestled alongside shoppers perusing the greeting card aisle.

While the drugstore soda fountain is sadly no longer a concept we see very often, it stood as a staple on many a Main Street, USA. A throwback to simpler times of sipping root beer and nickel tabs, they flourished around the turn of the twentieth century. At the time, the sodas were concocted by the pharmacists and included medicinal recipes, including ingredients like cocaine, legal then, for energy. Ice cream was added, along with sweetened milk and raw egg, to create soda creams and milkshakes.

Eventually, a pharmacist created an actual soda fountain, which became popular in drugstores across the country. This led to the invention of soda dispensers, replacing the "soda jerk" employee and allowing for syrups and preset recipes to move out from behind the back counters and into the mainstream. Brands like Coca-Cola and Dr. Pepper began bottling their recipes, and the need and novelty of the pharmacy soda fountain waned. Today, it is rare to find a luncheonette within the walls of a drugstore, but soda can be purchased far and wide.

At Green's, you can enjoy pancakes or a club sandwich, or sip on an egg cream. The menu is simple with tried and true classics, as is the décor, with checkered flooring and no frills tables and chairs. The shop offers a variety of convenience goods from shampoo to sunscreen in a nostalgic setting. Celebrities like Jimmy Buffet may pop by, and the daily crowd includes all walks of life on the island, looking to stock up on cold medicine, snag a copy of *The Shiny Sheet*, or enjoy an afternoon bite.

Address 151 N County Road, Palm Beach, FL 33480, +1 (561) 832-0304, www.greenspb.com | Getting there From I-95: Take exit 71 and drive east on Palm Beach Lakes Boulevard to Florida A1A North/Flagler Memorial Bridge. Continue on N County Road. Pharmacy and parking on the right. | Hours See website for luncheonette and pharmacy hours | Tip Visit Delray Shores, the longest-standing, family-owned, independent pharmacy in Delray Beach (124 NE 5th Avenue, Delray Beach, www.delrayshorespharmacy.com).

52 Harriet Himmel Theater
To have and to hold, pray or punch

What is now the Harriet Himmel Theater at the center of Rosemary Square was built in 1926 as the First United Methodist Church. The grand, two-story structure features a barrel tile roof, copper bell tower, and large clock face overlooking the main plaza of the square. The Spanish tile staircase leading to the arched, windowed, pecky cypress doorways of the entrance is a focal point of countless photographs and has ushered many newlyweds into the world through crowds of sparklers, rice, and bubbles.

The Harriet Himmel Theater has transitioned through many uses throughout its lifetime, originally constructed as an upgrade from the First United Methodists' 1898 wooden chapel. In 1928, the theater was used to house victims of the Great Okeechobee Hurricane. The church eventually struggled with debt in the wake of the depression and left the building. It has since seen almost a century of development in the surrounding space. For over a decade, CityPlace operated here as an outdoor, multi-use community of residential condominiums, office space, dining, retail, and entertainment before being renamed Rosemary Square in 2019. One of the few buildings spared during the redevelopment of the area in the 1990s, the Harriet Himmel Gilman Theater was repurposed as a 350-seat theater and event venue accommodating up to 500 people. In 2005, Harriet Himmel won a divorce settlement and removed her ex-husband's name from the theater, thus bestowing its present name.

Known for its remarkable entrance, vaulted ceilings, archways, and overall architectural significance, it is a historical venue for religious events, performances, and social events. While it is regarded as a cultural hub, the theater has also hosted proms, bar/bat mitzvahs, and even mixed martial arts fight nights. As of 2020, it returned to its roots as a place of congregation for Christ Fellowship Church.

Address 700 S Rosemary Avenue, West Palm Beach, FL 33401, +1 (561) 231-6044, www.facebook.com/harriethimmeltheater | **Getting there** From I-95: Take exit 70 and drive east on Okeechobee Boulevard. Turn left onto S Rosemary Avenue. Location and parking are on the right. | **Hours** See website for hours | **Tip** Explore Rosemary Square with pop up concepts like The Garden Shoppe selling living plants and original artworks by Sarah LaPierre (600 S Rosemary Avenue, Unit 168, West Palm Beach, www.pbfarmyards.org).

53__Havana's 24-Hour Window

Caffeine and croquetas around the clock

A family tradition for over 25 years, Havana Cuban Restaurant is on its third generation of the Reyes/Perez family. Known for their 24-hour window offering an abbreviated menu, coffee, and espresso-based beverages, Havana has become a landmark along Dixie Highway. The interior restaurant is open seven days a week for lunch and dinner, serving up Cuban classics, like *arroz con pollo* and *ropa vieja*, alongside the aroma of fresh Cuban bread coated in garlic butter spread. The award-winning *cafe con leche* with hot espresso and steamed milk is a must, with a piece of gooey *tres leches* cake.

A stomping ground for regulars that is equally friendly to newcomers, the window, or *ventanita*, at Havana is a place to step up and make your order heard. There's not a true line here – the window is first come first served, with a steady stream throughout the day. But wait to start sampling your treats until you're out of the crowd to avoid getting them jostled right out of your hands (regulars call that "flying croquetas"). The ladies of the *ventanita* know customers by name and their usual orders. Some customers have become employees over the years, and others are there frequently enough that you'd think they work here. Inside, the kitchen is run by a team of cooks, rather than a chef, who learned the recipes from the late Roberto Reyes. The menu is modeled after his childhood memories of food.

Rich with Cuban heritage and famous for their Cuban sandwich, Havana has served celebrities ranging from Bob Dylan, Paul Newman, and Bonnie Raitt to Zsa Zsa Gabor, Sofia Vergara, and Martha Stewart. The menu is not meant to reflect Cuban food as seen in Miami, but to translate the family's homeland experience with a soft tailoring to the South Florida market. A long-standing gem, Havana is a Cuban corner in the heart of Palm Beach County.

Address 6801 S Dixie Highway, West Palm Beach, FL 33405, +1 (561) 547-9799, www.havanacubanfood.com | **Getting there** From I-95: Take exit 66 and drive east on Forest Hill Boulevard. Restaurant and parking on right at the intersection of US Highway 1. | **Hours** Window open 24 hours; Restaurant Sun–Thu 11am–10pm, Fri & Sat 11am–11pm | **Tip** Just down the street is Don Ramon's, which opened just three years before Havana and is also locally famous for their Cuban cuisine (7101 S Dixie Highway, West Palm Beach, www.donramonrestaurant.com).

54 HEAU Mural

The beauty under the bridge

Below the flow of traffic passing over the Royal Park Bridge is a hidden treasure named HEAU. Created by Sean Yoro, known in the art world as "HULA," this stunning public mural graces the bridge wall just above the water. Originally from Oahu, self-taught HULA moved to New York to pursue his talents in fine arts. He has made a name for himself by painting women featured along the waterline, oftentimes painting while balancing on a stand-up paddleboard. HULA is noted for creating an environmental discussion through his works, as they are commonly found on otherwise forgotten spaces or structures. His pieces are typically oil paintings made with strictly non-toxic media.

HEAU was inspired by the idea of being "confined to our own boxes." The image was modeled by a friend named Clara using a cardboard box in a Brooklyn studio. The resulting image under the bridge measures 23 feet high and 20 feet across, with the tide adjusting how exposed the subject is. The completion of this particular fan-favorite piece was threatened when vandals stole the artist's supplies and threw glass bottles, creating an unsafe working area early in the process. Luckily, Yoro was able to replace his equipment and finish the painting.

HEAU was actually the first "legal" mural by HULA. The artwork was produced as part of CANVAS West Palm Beach in November 2015. Considered the country's largest outdoor museum show, downtown areas come to life during the annual CANVAS calendar as a collection of innovative artists from all over the world transform public spaces. Founded by Nicole Henry, the multi-week event includes temporary and permanent artwork and installations. Down the heart of Clematis Street and throughout surrounding streets, as well as the city of Lake Worth, visitors can find public works by Zeus, Kobra, Greg Mike, WRDSMTH, and Lonac, among others.

Address Royal Park Bridge, South Flagler Drive and Lakeview Avenue, www.byhula.com |
Getting there From I-95: Take exit 70 and drive east on Okeechobee Boulevard about three
miles. Royal Park Bridge is at the intersection of South Flagler Drive. Street parking. |
Hours Unrestricted | **Tip** Visit CANVAS maps to view installations, including several at the
corner of Clematis Street and Narcissus Avenue (www.canvasmuseum.org).

55 H. G. Roosters
Where being a drag is being the life of the party

Just south of downtown lies a place where "everyone is welcome – and no one is bored." Welcome to H. G. Roosters, the longest-running gay bar in Florida since 1984. This friendly establishment has been at the epicenter of the LGBTQ+ community for over 30 years. Known for their weekly programming, including the award-winning Saturday night drag show, Roosters offers an array of lively activities, from bingo, to billiards, to lip sync battles.

The longtime success of Roosters can be attributed to those who have called it home. Late bar manager Michael "La La" Brown was the heart of the local gay community before his tragic murder in 2008. He served as a board member of the South Florida chapter of the NAMES Project and toured with the AIDS Memorial Quilt made to celebrate the lives of people who died from AIDS-related causes. He inspired the Compass Community Center (see ch. 101) and served as the grand marshal at the city's 1997 Gay Pride Parade. Brown also provided an outlet for HIV outreach, raised funds for Mother's Cupboard, sponsored PrideFest, and received the Fundraiser Extraordinaire Award.

Melissa St. John, known as "First Lady of the Palm Beaches" or Charles Capers off stage, is the award-winning host of the popular Saturday night show. Named by *South Florida Gay News'* "Out 50" as one of the most influential members of the LGBTQ+ community, St. John is an adored activist and an advocate for those affected by HIV / AIDS. She has also served as grand marshal of Palm Beach Pride and raised countless funds in her humanitarian efforts.

The fact is that H. G. Roosters has been a place of refuge, hope, support, and belonging for the LGBTQ+ community of South Florida and beyond. After a fire ravaged the venue in 2020, the community soon came to the rescue with shows of support and donations to help the owners rebuild this rooster from its ashes.

Address 823 Belvedere Road, West Palm Beach, FL 33401, +1 561.832.9119, www.roosterswpb.com | **Getting there** From I-95: Take exit 69A and drive east on Belvedere Boulevard for about 0.5 mile. Bar is on the left. | **Hours** Mon–Thu 3pm–3am, Fri & Sat 3pm–4am, Sun 3pm–3am | **Tip** Don't miss Werk It Out Wednesday drag shows at the popular live music venue Propaganda in Lake Worth (6 S J Street, Lake Worth, www.propagandalw.com).

56 Hoffman's Chocolates
Welcome to the sweet side of life

In 1975, a very sweet and simple idea led to the creation of the largest chocolate manufacturer in the State of Florida. Paul Hoffman borrowed just over 1,000 dollars to purchase a modest candy shop so that he could make confections and enjoy time with his family. He studied chocolate, investigated ingredients, and tested methods, resulting in a product that became a legacy. Half a century later, Hoffman's Chocolates can be found in grocery stores and at over half a dozen locations throughout South Florida.

The 15,000-square-foot Bavarian chalet that currently houses Hoffman's Chocolates is in stark contrast to the original Lake Worth location that was a fraction of the size. The factory boasts a 30-foot picture window allowing tourgoers a peek into the day-to-day creation of the over-seventy varieties of handmade confections. A large retail shop complete with an ice cream counter gives you the opportunity to taste the treats creating the sweet aroma circulating through the property. Displays of fan favorites, such as chocolate covered pretzels, seasonal holiday baskets, and glass cases of barks and jitterbugs, give you ideas inside, while the gardens cover the outdoor area.

Famous for their Winter Wonderland, the gardens are adorned with over 100,000 lights, inflatable characters, Christmas trees, menorahs – and sometimes even a skating rink – each year during the month of December.

Hoffman's Chocolates invites locals and tourists alike to visit the Greenacres factory for tastings, shopping, guided tours, and chocolatier classes. Paul Hoffman's vision continues to influence new recipes, maintaining the use of the fresh, high-quality ingredients that made his chocolate famous so many years ago. Enjoy chocolates and caramels in all shapes and sizes, from cream-filled truffles and chocolate-covered cookies to peanut brittle and caramel corn.

Address 5190 Lake Worth Road, Greenacres, FL 33463, +1 (561) 967-2213, www.hoffmans.com, support@Hoffmans.com | **Getting there** From I-95: Take exit 63 and drive west on 6th Avenue South. Turn right on S Congress Avenue, then left on Lake Worth Road. Factory and parking are on the left. | **Hours** Mon–Sat 11am–7pm, Sun noon–6pm | **Tip** Meet the innovative chocolate makers at 5150 Chocolate bean-to-bar chocolate factory (1010 N Federal Highway, Delray Beach, www.5150chocolate.com).

57__ The Kennedy Pew

Don't answer the red phone

With its stunning architecture and award-winning historical preservation, St. Edward Catholic Church is a sight to behold. Designed in the Spanish Renaissance style featuring towers, bronze doors ,and a Spanish tile roof, the interior of the 1926 church displays hand-painted ceilings, stained-glass windows, fresco paintings, and a Carrara marble altar. The original glory of the property was restored in the 2000s, earning the church two of the area's most prestigious awards for historical preservation, The Ballinger Award from The Preservation Foundation of Palm Beach and The Knott Award from the Historical Society of Palm Beach County.

St. Edward was the place of worship for the Kennedys during their Palm Beach visits. A red phone was even installed in the back of the church during JFK's presidency should a crisis arise during Mass. His favorite pew is marked with a plaque reading *President John F. Kennedy knelt here at mass.*

In 1960, the church was one of the places where Richard Paul Pavlick stalked the Kennedy family.

Three years before Lee Harvey Oswald assassinated John F. Kennedy in Texas, police discovered and thwarted an assassination attempt in Palm Beach. One of Pavlick's initial plans was to blow up the church during mass with Kennedy in attendance. He later decided on the Kennedy residence but did not execute his plan to detonate dynamite when he saw First Lady Jacqueline and their children within striking distance. Kennedy spent his last weekend in Palm Beach before the fatal Dallas motorcade shooting on November 22, 1963. However, he attended St. Ann Catholic Church that final Sunday.

St. Edward is home to several treasures including a six-foot statue of *The Sacred Heart of Jesus* and relief of *The Last Supper* carved from solid Carrara marble and a four-foot, two thousand pound statue of Jesus Christ carved from limestone.

Address 144 N County Road, Palm Beach, FL 33480, +1 (561)832.0400, www.stedwardpb.com | Getting there From I-95: Take exit 70 and drive east on Okeechobee Boulevard. Cross bridge onto island. Turn left on S County Road. Church is on the left. | Hours See website for mass schedules | Tip Palm Beach Synagogue is located one block south on Sunset Avenue with a beautiful arched window façade (120 N County Road, Palm Beach, www.palmbeachsynagogue.org).

58 Kravis Center Organ

The million dollar, one-of-a-kind sound machine

The Raymond F. Kravis Center for the Performing Arts is the epicenter of theater in Palm Beach County. A true testament to the persistence of the arts community and their determination to create a major performing arts center, the Kravis is the result of decades of plans, fundraising, and pivoting to make it happen. The eventual home of the Kravis was originally a baseball facility. For over half a century, Wright Field, later renamed Connie Mack Field after the Hall of Famer, hosted spring training for the Philadelphia Athletics and St. Louis Browns. A plaque marking the placement of home plate can still be found on the property, where baseball greats like Babe Ruth, Lou Gehrig, Jackie Robinson, Joe DiMaggio, and Mickey Mantle once stepped up to bat.

Since 1992, the center has stood on its 10-acre perch, delighting attendees with a range of performances. Thanks to a 2016 gift from board member and major area arts supporter Alexander W. Dreyfoos, theatergoers now experience the one-of-a-kind digital George W. Mergens Memorial Organ. The $1.5-million custom instrument can recreate the sound of some of the greatest organs in the world through the sampling of over 300 sounds collected from almost three dozen pipe organs. All in all, the organ is capable of reproducing approximately 18,000 sounds.

The center offers a year-round schedule featuring hundreds of shows, from Broadway classics, to ballet, to stand-up comedy. The over-2,000-seat Alexander W. Dreyfoos, Jr. Concert Hall hosts a gamut of performances alongside the more intimate Marshall E. Rinker, Sr. Playhouse, and Helen K. Persson Hall. Named in honor of Raymond F. Kravis, a prominent geologist and philanthropist, at the $7-million contribution of his friends the center also provides an outlet for Alexander W. Dreyfoos School of the Arts, Miami City Ballet, and Palm Beach Symphony.

Address 701 Okeechobee Boulevard, West Palm Beach, FL 33401, +1 (561) 832-7469, www.kravis.org | Getting there From I-95: Take exit 70 and drive east on Okeechobee Boulevard. Theater is on the left, valet and garage parking available. | Hours See website for performance schedule | Tip Theater lovers can enjoy a show in the intimate setting of Palm Beach Dramaworks just down the road (201 Clematis Street, West Palm Beach, www.palmbeachdramaworks.org).

59__ The Leopard Lounge
Hidden erotica if you know where to look

Known for its live entertainment and phenomenal people-watching, Leopard Lounge is an iconic Palm Beach hotspot, located within the Chesterfield Hotel. While it has been known as the Chesterfield since 1989, if the walls of this 1926 hotel could talk, they would have quite the stories to tell. And they'd probably be talking about the ceiling of the Leopard Lounge.

Painted by local artist Lino Mario under a pen name in the 1990s and while standing on top of the piano, the luscious ladies of his ceiling artwork feature the faces of aristocrats of his day. At first glance the design takes on an abstract swirling pattern but with a closer look the paint strokes tell a much steamier story. The imagery also features a self-indulgent, well-endowed self portrait of the artist within the sensual depiction. The artwork was completed over the course of a year and a half – for the whopping price tag of his bartab.

The ceiling suits the grand décor of the lounge, with its black lacquer walls, beveled mirrors, gold hardware, leather seating and pops of leopard print. Punkah fans give a tropical breeze while the rich tones create an intimate and discrete atmosphere appealing to decades of celebrities ranging from Jimmy Fallon and Drew Barrymore to Tina Louise and Patti LaBelle. The bar proudly serves 14 martini variations which help prepare the crowd for a night on the dance floor with live music filling the space six nights a week.

The Chesterfield Hotel opened in 1926 as Lido-Venice before becoming the Vineta, Royal Park, and Palm Court. The current ownership, Red Carnation Collection, brings a luxury pedigree to the property with world renowned service. The four-star boutique hotel offers 53 guest rooms bringing English charm to the island but expect to see locals, especially old money, grace the seats of Leopard Lounge where happy hour meets true sophistication.

Address 363 Cocoanut Row, Palm Beach, FL 33480, +1 (561) 659-5800, www.chesterfieldpb.com | Getting there From I-95: Take exit 70 and drive east on Okeechobee Boulevard about three miles. Cross the bridge over the Intracoastal Waterway onto Royal Palm Way. Turn right onto Cocoanut Row. Hotel is on left. Street parking and complimentary valet available. | Hours See website for hours | Tip Book high tea at the Chesterfield for a true English experience in the library or courtyard (363 Cocoanut Row, Palm Beach).

60 Lilly Pulitzer Design
Palm Beach's main squeeze on Worth Avenue

One of the most celebrated names and fashion houses of South Florida, Lilly Pulitzer is eye-catching, recognizable, and embraced by those who adore all things Palm Beach. The flagship store, located on Worth Avenue, marked the brand's return to the island and features a design studio, where shoppers are able to interact with an artist creating prints on-site and leave with a customized piece like the iconic shift dress.

The birth of the Lilly Pulitzer brand is so very Palm Beach. Lillian McKim of Standard Oil ties was married to publishing heir Herbert "Peter" Pulitzer who, within his portfolio, owned several Florida citrus groves. After a short stint in a psychiatric hospital, the clinically bored socialite decided to open a juice stand in Via Mizner (see ch. 50) as a side project. After ruining her wardrobe with splotches of yellow lemon, green lime, pink grapefruit, and orange juice, she started designing and wearing shift dresses that concealed the splashes. Her new fashion sense, which was very different from the girdled and fitted look of the 1950s, attracted other ladies of the island, and juice stand customers began requesting shifts of their own.

Pulitzer soon went from finding remnants at local thrift shops to having Key West Hand Print Fabrics create commissioned bolts, though it was rumored that the fateful Jackie Kennedy shift that propelled the brand's popularity was fashioned from kitchen curtains. Before she knew it, Lilly Pulitzer had created an authentic American resort wear empire with a cult following the brand continues to enjoy.

Launched in 2018, this flagship store was meticulously designed with custom build outs, one-of-a-kind, hand-painted fitting rooms, and a bar for serving parched patrons. The bright white and gold backdrop allows the prints to pop throughout the space and provides a gallery-like quality for freshly painted designs to dry.

Address 240 Worth Avenue, Palm Beach, FL 33480, +1 (561) 653-8282, www.lillypulitzer.com, worthavenue@lillypulitzer.com | Getting there From I-95: Take exit 70 and drive east on Okeechobee Boulevard about three miles. Cross the bridge over the Intracoastal Waterway onto Royal Palm Way. Turn right onto S County Road, then right onto Worth Avenue. Store is on the left, street parking available. | Hours Mon–Sat 10am–6pm, Sun noon–5pm | Tip Stroll down Worth Avenue to D Dream Atelier to visit the location of Pulitzer's original juice stand and shop (23 Via Mizner, Palm Beach, www.ddreamatelier.com).

61 Little Red Schoolhouse
Turn of the century education

Stepping up to the double front door of this simple, one-room, red wooden structure is to be transported into the 19th century. A place for the younger generation to experience "living history," the Little Red Schoolhouse was the first permanent school built in Southeast Florida. While it initially held class in West Palm Beach, this landmark now stands just steps from the ocean, fully restored, at Phipps Ocean Park.

School was first in session at the Little Red Schoolhouse at its original location in 1886. A handful of children under the age of 17 gathered for instruction from then just 16-year-old Hattie Gale of Kansas. At the time, what is now West Palm Beach was part of an expansive Dade County, with very little connected development. The county provided the school district with a $200 grant to construct the 880-square-foot building. Locals donated their time to cover labor expenses, while the Ladies Aid Society sold embroidered linens to help furnish the school.

Within the first decade, class sizes had grown to over 30 children. Students arrived any way they could travel, whether by boat or on foot. But by the turn of the century, the school was no longer being used and was relocated to the property of John Phipps, who used it as an outdoor shed. In the 1960s, the estate was demolished, but the schoolhouse was saved and moved to the park.

The Little Red Schoolhouse now provides a backdrop for students as part of the Living History program, where fourth graders from surrounding counties can experience a day in the life of a late 1800s pupil. An abbreviated day includes learning arithmetic, reading, and writing in the style of Spencerian script, while participating in pioneer recess and educational activities. The site is only open to school classes, but anyone can visit from the outside and imagine life as a child during the earliest days of Palm Beach.

Welcome, Scholars.   March , 1886
Good posture makes good thinkers.

1) 13+14−15=
2) 160−25+10=
3) 213+152+73=
4) 3,513+3562=
5) 7,856−3,451=
6) 7,518−2,036=

7) 5×4+3=
8) 8×9−10=
9) 247×10=
10) (13+5)÷3=
11) (7×9)÷3=
12) 54÷(3×3)=

Address 2185 S Ocean Boulevard, Palm Beach, FL 33480, +1 (561) 832-0731, www.palmbeachpreservation.org/visit/little-red-schoolhouse | **Getting there** From I-95: Take exit 68 and drive east on Southern Boulevard. Cross over the bridge onto the island. Turn right on S Ocean Boulevard. Park and parking are on the left. | **Hours** Unrestricted from the outside | **Tip** While at Phipps Ocean Park, enjoy the beach access and snorkeling, or hit the courts at the Phipps Tennis Center (2201 S Ocean Boulevard, Palm Beach, www.townofpalmbeach.com).

62 Lorikeet Loft
This place is for the birds

Within the gates of the Palm Beach Zoo and Conservation Society enter Lorikeet Loft, an aviary with approximately 40 birds. Filled with botanicals and navigated by a circular walkway, guests can purchase nectar cups to attract the smaller, rainbow-colored parrots out of the greenery. These friendly and affectionate birds are indigenous to Australia and are feathered in vibrant shades of blue, green, red, and yellow. Their beaks brighten from black to orange as they mature, living up to 30 years old.

Opened in 2017, the loft is an experiential addition to the 23-acre zoo which houses over 500 animals featuring an array of birds from roseate spoonbills to bald eagles, excitable howler monkeys, regal tigers, the endangered Florida panther, and alligators, including a rare leucistic white gator named Mardi. The Palm Beach Zoo has a robust conservation and biodiversity program, with research efforts in Bolivia, Malaysia, and right here with endangered zoo residents like Fiona, the Panamanian jaguar.

The zoo has seen many transformations since its inception in the 1950s, when Parks Superintendent Paul Dreher built a red barn and filled it with a handful of goats, ducks, chickens, and a goose. Known as "The Johnny Appleseed of Palm Beach County," Dreher became the namesake of Dreher Park after he helped bring about the purchasing of then-Bacon Park from the State of Florida. The $100 transaction helped see the landfill become a functional park, which now houses the zoo.

Families enjoy the zoo not only for the animals but also the interactive play fountain, where kids can be found splashing about in swimsuits, the nature play pavilion filled with creative outdoor play areas, and the Tropics Café restaurant overlooking a lagoon of pink Chilean flamingos. Guests can enjoy a ride on the carousel, catch a show, or enjoy keepers' educational talks.

Address 1301 Summit Boulevard, West Palm Beach, FL 33405, +1 (561) 547-9453, www.palmbeachzoo.org | Getting there From I-95: Take exit 68 and drive east on Southern Boulevard. Turn right on Parker Avenue. Turn right on Summit Boulevard, then right on Dreher Trail North. Zoo and parking on the left. | Hours Daily 9am–5pm | Tip Travel south to Coconut Creek to visit Butterfly World, featuring butterfly aviaries and gardens (Tradewinds Park, 3600 West Sample Road, Coconut Creek, www.butterflyworld.com).

63   Lost Weekend

Game night for grownups at the "bar-cade"

Entering Lost Weekend, patrons are greeted with a line of billiards tables alongside foosball, table shuffleboard, and skeeball. Vintage arcade games line the wall from Ms. PacMan, to Mortal Kombat, to a claw crane full of plush toys, while a full bar runs alongside the opposing wall. But don't let the childhood favorites fool you. This "bar-cade" is a pool hall and playground for adults, with cold beers on tap and late night vibes. The concept has been a staple since its 1995 opening on Olive Avenue, later moving to its current location in 2014.

Located in the 500 block of Clematis Street, Lost Weekend is a piece of a larger puzzle. The vision of Rodney Mayo of Subculture Group and Maurice Costigan of O'Shea's, there is something different about this segment of the downtown scene. Built around community, Subculture Coffee acts as a meeting place for hustling entrepreneurs, while lunch dates pop into Kapow Noodle Bar and move into happy hour hotspots like Hullabaloo. Pizza by the slice is offered at Clematis Pizza, and weekly programming like trivia and live music are held at O'Shea's Pub. The venues collaborate to host St. Patrick's Day block parties, MoonFest at Halloween, and weekend 500 BLK events. Together the "500 block" has become a cultural center, popular among millennials and others seeking connectivity.

Dimly lit with a dive bar feel and hints of nostalgia, Lost Weekend stands as an entertainment and nightlife venue within the mix. El Segundo Café serves gourmet-style tacos from a back counter, and bartenders shake up the main game room. Some come for the DJ, others for a game of eight ball. The crowd usually begins at happy hour and builds from there. Be sure to stock up on quarters to fuel the tables, games, and jukebox. For a change of pace, head upstairs to the swanky Voltaire lounge for music, sushi, and cocktails.

Address 526 Clematis Street, West Palm Beach, FL 33401, +1 (561) 293-2786, www.sub-culture.org | Getting there From I-95: Take exit 70 and drive east on Okeechobee Boulevard. Turn left on S Quadrille Boulevard, then left on Clematis Street. The destination is on the left. Street parking available. | Hours Daily 4pm–2am | Tip Head down Clematis Street to Camelot for Kennedy-inspired nightlife (114 S Narcissus Avenue, West Palm Beach).

64   Mar-a-Lago
The grandest parties and murderous design

Mar-a-Lago is a 1920's historic landmark estate. The name means "sea to lake" due to the property's positioning between the Atlantic Ocean and Lake Worth. The latest owner, Donald Trump, purchased the property in 1985 and would later refer to it as the "Winter White House." The stunning compound has over 15 acres and an estate with more than 50 bedrooms – and three bomb shelters. But before it became part of the Trump empire, it was the home of Marjorie Merriweather Post of Post cereal fame.

While Post inherited much of her wealth, she blossomed as a businesswoman with the creation of General Foods through the acquisitions of multiple brands. Her marriage to stockbroker E. F. Hutton only increased her net worth and influence. In the 1920s, the power couple decided to purchase the Mar-a-Lago property and build a home. The timing proved to have a major impact on the design, as Marjorie pushed the limits in an effort to keep hundreds of laborers employed during the economic crisis.

The result was massive, ornate, and awe-inspiring. A fervent entertainer, Post hosted lavish parties – imagine the Ringling Brothers Circus or raucous square dancing. One of those parties' guest lists included "Mad Harry" Thaw and Evelyn Nesbit. Thaw had been found not guilty of the murder of New York architect Stanford White, by reason of insanity. Upon his arrival at Mar-a-Lago, he was overheard saying, "My God, I killed the wrong architect."

Upon Marjorie's death, she gifted Mar-a-Lago to the United States as a retreat for political elites and dignitaries. However, upkeep forced officials to return the property to her children, who eventually sold it to Donald Trump. Almost 30 years later, he inadvertently realized her dream by becoming the 45th president. You must be a member to enter, but you can still feel the spirit of its original grand hostess in the views of the building and grounds.

Address 1100 S Ocean Boulevard, Palm Beach, FL 33480, +1 (561) 832-2600, www.maralagoclub.com | Getting there From I-95: Take exit 68 and drive east on Southern Boulevard. Entrance and parking is located and on the left. | Hours Tue–Sat 7am–10pm, Sun 7am–3pm | Tip Don't miss Chef Clay Carne's tacos at nearby Cholo Soy. Dine in the back patio, surrounded by cheeky Virgin Mary and Speedy Gonzalez wall murals (3715 S Dixie Highway, West Palm Beach, www.cholosoycocina.com).

65 Mounts Botanical Garden

Walk on water at Windows on the Floating World

The oldest and largest botanical garden in the county, Mounts Botanical Gardens has been inspiring and educating through nature for over 40 years. Featuring more than 2,000 species of tropical and subtropical plants, the gardens offer an array of visitor experiences like the Garden of Tranquility, Sun Garden of Extremes, Butterfly Garden, Children's Maze, and the largest specialty garden, Windows on the Floating World.

Developed by artists Mags Harries and Lajos Héder in collaboration with Wantman Group Inc., Windows on the Floating World was led by the Art in Public Places program. The piece was designed to create an immersive experience for visitors and their senses by bringing them into the gardens and onto the water. Four-foot wide, open grid walkways span over wetlands, where guests can listen to falling water, watch wading birds, feed koi fish, smell the floral air, and view hundreds of species of plants, shrubs, trees, and foliage. The geometric pattern that outlines the "windows" allows sightseers to pass through, slowly meander or pause in reflection on top of the water.

The Blume Tropical Wetland Garden was named in honor of Margaret Blume, a local philanthropist who has shown her dedication and generosity to the community through various projects and donations, including Mounts, the Literacy Coalition of Palm Beach County, Cornell Art Museum, and the Rapa Nui Reef.

Mounts Botanical Garden welcomes guests daily for grounds exploration, guided tours and educational programming. The surroundings are ever-changing with rainfall fluctuation, seasonal blooms, and rotating exhibits. Depending on the time of year, the colors may include shades of yellow, orange, pink, red, or purple. For those looking to bring the vibrancy of the gardens home, volunteers maintain Mounts Nursery, which sells a selection of herbs, plants and shrubs three days a week.

Address 531 N Military Trail, West Palm Beach, FL 33415, +1 (561) 233-1757, www.mounts.org | Getting there From I-95: Take exit 68 and drive west on Southern Boulevard. Merge right onto Military Trail. Gardens and parking on the left. | Hours Daily 10am–4pm | Tip Keep an eye out for opportunities to visit the nearby Unbelievable Acres Botanical Gardens (470 63rd Trail North, West Palm Beach, www.unbelievableacresbotanicgardens.org).

66 Norton Museum of Art

Claude Monet's impressions of landscapes

A cultural icon of the area, Norton Museum of Art was founded in 1941. It underwent major renovations in 2018 and is now a towering structure, featuring *Typewriter Eraser, Scale X* (1999) by Claes Oldenburg and Coosje van Bruggen at the entrance – an eye-catching presence along the Dixie Corridor. The museum has a notable permanent collection and features special exhibits, programs, and events. One of the prized works of art here is the *Gardens of the Villa Moreno* (1884) by Claude Monet.

Monet was a French Impressionist painter best known for his *Les Nymphéas* series featuring over 200 works centered around water lilies. Inspired by the gardens of his home in Giverny, France, the paintings have influenced countless works by other artists, including Roy Lichtenstein, whose *Water Lilies with Cloud* (1992) can also be found at Norton Museum. The large-scale, six-panel series is composed of screen printed enamel on stainless steel with bold colors and patterns in pop art fashion. In 2016, an immersive video installation by Mark Fox, *Giverny: Journal of an Unseen Garden 2016*, debuted at the museum, capturing underwater imagery from below the water lilies. The oil-on-canvas *Gardens of the Villa Moreno* depicts the landscape and architecture of Bordighera, Italy near the French border.

Norton Museum of Art itself is the legacy of the late Ralph Hubbard Norton and his wife Elizabeth Calhoun Norton. Art lovers in their personal lives, they amassed a vast collection of paintings and sculptures during their time in Chicago. When they retired to the West Palm Beach area, they decided to open the museum as an outlet to share their personal collection and bring the first fine arts museum to South Florida. Norton has been a focal point of the local art scene through exhibits, educational programs, awards, and on-site event programming, including Art After Dark.

Address 1450 S Dixie Highway, West Palm Beach, FL 33401, +1 (561) 832-5196, www.norton.org, info@norton.org | **Getting there** From I-95: Take exit 70 and drive east on Okeechobee Boulevard. Turn right on US Highway 1. Museum located on the right, parking across the street. | **Hours** Mon–Thu & Sat 10am–5pm, Fri 10am–10pm, Sun 11am–5pm | **Tip** Walk the gardens and tour the historic property at the nearby Norton House and Ann Norton Sculpture Gardens (253 Barcelona Road, West Palm Beach, www.ansg.org).

67 Okeeheelee Park

Professional grade outdoor play

Within the 1,700 acres that make Okeeheelee Park one of the largest parks in South Florida is a collection of professional-level courses designed for the most discerning sports competitors. Situated alongside recreational facilities for the casual participant, these tracks bring an elevated style of play and, for card and permit holders, provide top-notch training and competition facilities.

Okeeheelee BMX Track provides over 1,000 feet of skilled track that has been ranked in the top five in the country and taken the top spot in the state for multiple years. USA BMX members can be found practicing their skills and competing alongside fellow riders on a rippling course of berms and turns.

Then there's Greg Norman Jr.'s Shark Wake Park 561, located within the perimeter of the park, offering beginner and advanced cable systems that replicate watersports that you'd normally need a boat to pursue. Children – and adults acting like kids – traverse Obstacle Island, the largest floating obstacle course on the East Coast, while adventure seekers enjoy wakeboarding, knee boarding, water skiing, wake skating, and foil boarding on the course.

Okeeheelee Park also offers casual activities, from stocked pier fishing to pickleball, and tennis courts to multipurpose fields. Disc golfers hit the links, dogs cavort in Pooch Pines, and hikers explore the surrounding nature trails. Water skiers glide atop the lake and take flight from ramps (their boats are required to have proper permitting and safety equipment). Picnic areas and pavilions provide shelter for grilling, while the Nature Center hosts educational classes and offers rental facilities.

Three par-nine golf courses converge at the pro shop that offers club rentals and public play. The sheer size of this park, coupled with the ample amenities, make this a playground for young and old, visitors and locals alike.

Address 7715 Forest Hill Boulevard, West Palm Beach, FL 33413, +1 (561) 966-6600, www.okeeheeleepark.com, web@okeeheeleepark.com | Getting there From I-95: Take exit 66 and drive west on Forest Hill Boulevard for about six miles. Park and parking on the left. | Hours Daily dawn–dusk | Tip The Jim Brandon Equestrian Center hosts miles of riding trails surrounding the training rings, covered arena, and stables. The world-class facility covers over 100 acres and can house over 125 horses (7500 Forest Hill Boulevard, West Palm Beach).

68 Palm Beach Clock Tower
The gateway to Worth Avenue

The Palm Beach Clock Tower greets visitors entering the world famous Worth Avenue. Built only in 2010, the 25-foot-tall coquina tower quickly became one of the most iconic images for the island of Palm Beach. With a clock face on each of its four sides, the tower was part of an approximately $15-million renovation project of Worth Avenue. Standing in place of the former Palm Beach Pier, the clock tower presides over Chanel, Tiffany & Co., Gucci, and Jimmy Choo, among hundreds of designer and boutique storefronts along four blocks.

For nearly a century, Worth Avenue has captivated the eyes of the wealthy. Kassatly's, the street's first shop, opened in 1923, selling linens, sportswear, and curated goods. In 1926, Saks Fifth Avenue expanded its flagship operation from New York City to open its second location at 300 Worth. Lilly Pulitzer got her start selling shift dresses from her juice shop (see ch. 60), and Addison Mizner lived in a via just off the avenue (see ch. 50). The vias of Worth Avenue are famous in their own right, like an escape into a European courtyard, with their colorful tiles, fountains, and open shop doors. While shoppers can be seen strolling the avenue year-round today, Worth Avenue began as a seasonal activity of the "Cottage Colony," where the rich and famous wintered in their resort-like cottages along the beach from New Year's to the Washington's Birthday Ball each February. You can still find many of the stores that opened in the early days and shop for the finest luxury goods.

Designed by Mark Marsh, the domed clock tower is a popular meeting point and photo backdrop. The coral stone monument also includes a plaque paying homage to the fallen pier that once stood here. (Sadly the plaque has frequently gone missing due to theft.) Across from the tower are two stone pillars branded, "Worth Avenue," framing the one-way street's grand entrance.

Address 423 S Ocean Boulevard, Palm Beach, FL 33480, www.worth-avenue.com, info@worth-avenue.com | Getting there From I-95: Take exit 70 toward E Okeechobee Boulevard. Continue on Okeechobee Boulevard. Turn right onto S County Road, then left onto Hammon Avenue. Turn left onto S Ocean Boulevard. The Clock Tower is on the right. Park near Worth Avenue on the left. | Hours Unrestricted | Tip Visit the Via Parigi Piazza off Worth Avenue, named in honor of Paris Singer, an early resident, philanthropist, and heir to the founder of the Singer Sewing Company (Via Parigi, Palm Beach).

69 _ Palm Beach Garage

Cars in the corridor of collectibles

Over 40 antique stores line the Dixie Corridor to create Antique Row. Gaining national acclaim, the stores provide an opportunity for window shopping and offer enthusiasts access to an eclectic selection of antiques, art, and specialty goods. The antiques featured along the row date back to the 17th century, with carefully curated accessories and furnishings. The artwork ranges to contemporary with diverse influence and appeal. This section of roadway and history isn't just for shopping, with restaurants and services like auctioneers, appraisers, and Palm Beach Garage.

Palm Beach Garage specializes in classic automobiles, from sleek red Ferraris to canvas-topped Jollys. The prestigious garage caters to those looking to store and restore their vintage vehicles. The work of Jason Rosenzweig, the facility gives a nod to the allure of customer care of the past, while providing a modern level of top-notch service. Walking the rows of cars, you may see memorable wheels, like the Lincoln Continental from *The Godfather* or a re-imagined electric British icon, the Moke. These street-legal, low-speed vehicles combine electric power with a look designed for fun – just perfect for cruising along Palm Beach. They are available in a variety of colors from white to hot pink.

Antique Row has become a mecca for interior decorators looking to score collectibles at a reasonable price. Drawing from Palm Beach estates while saving on lower overhead costs, the location serves the antiquing community well. Shoppers can find success, whether they are in the market for a statement chandelier, a hand-carved armchair, or a vintage culinary poster. Due to the variety of businesses, there is a plethora of goods and services from clothing to framing, making this a notable stop that has gained the attention of celebrities from Cameron Diaz to Whoopi Goldberg and publications like *Travel + Leisure* magazine.

Address 3215 S Dixie Highway, West Palm Beach, FL 33405, +1 (561) 833-6622, www.westpalmbeachantiques.com | **Getting there** From I-95: Take exit 70 and drive east on Okeechobee Boulevard. Turn right on US Highway 1. Garage and parking on the right. | **Hours** Mon–Fri 8am–5pm | **Tip** Dixie Grill and Brewery features floor to – literally – ceiling antiques and collectibles to take in while you eat or sip one of their house beers (5101 S Dixie Highway, West Palm Beach, www.dixiegrillandbar.com).

70 Palm Beach Improv

Fresh material and big laughs on a small stage

Palm Beach Improv serves as a home for local and national comedians to take center stage. Basking in a big city comedy club atmosphere, guests are treated to an evening of laughs and libations in front of the famed brick wall backdrop. Grab a ticket to see local newcomers or top national tours in an intimate setting with a themed food menu and cocktail list.

The Improv has a rich history in the comedic world. Founded by Budd Friedman in 1963 in New York City as The Improvisation, it was originally a venue for Broadway performers to relax after a show. Most evenings, the Improv was filled with the camaraderie of singers and dancers until one night when Dave Astor decided to take the stage to test new material for his comedic act. Comedians soon followed suit, and the lineup transitioned from tunes to jokes. Comedy greats like Lily Tomlin, Jay Leno, and Andy Kaufman went to extreme lengths to get noticed and have their set picked up by Budd. The list of future stars that made early cameos is staggering. Imagine Barry Manilow on the piano with Dustin Hoffman subbing in during breaks. In the 1970s, Friedman decided to expand the Improv brand and opened a second location in Hollywood, California. The success was equal, with a new set of West Coast soon-to-be headliners taking the stage. In the early 2000s, a new expansion led to Improv locations throughout the US, eventually adding a stage in West Palm Beach.

Palm Beach Improv opened in 2001, immediately becoming the premier live comedy venue in the area. Celebrity acts like Chris Rock and Kevin Hart have been known to test new material locally in the smaller market before working it into their national acts. Most shows are 21 and over, with a two-drink minimum, plus a handful of 18-and-over showtimes. The Improv has a no heckler policy, boasts a packed schedule, and offers private event space.

Address 550 S Rosemary Avenue, Unit 250, West Palm Beach, FL 33401, +1 (561) 833-1812, www.palmbeachimprov.com, info@palmbeachimprov.com | **Getting there** From I-95: Take exit 70 and drive east on Okeechobee Boulevard. Turn left on Rosemary Avenue. Street and garage parking available. | **Hours** See website for events schedule | **Tip** For live music before or after a show, stop by next door at Copper Blues (550 S Rosemary Avenue, West Palm Beach, www.copperblueslive.com).

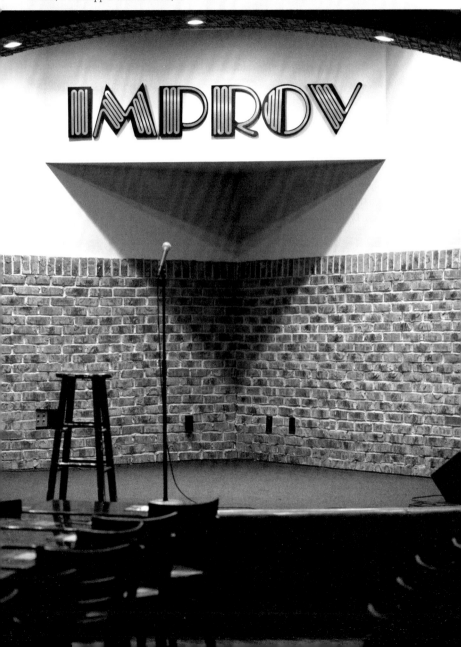

CENTRAL COUNTY

71 Palm Beach Par 3
Keeping it short but very sweet

Nestled between the Atlantic Ocean and Intracoastal Waterway, the Palm Beach Par 3 Golf Course has twice been named "The Best Par 3 in the US" by *Golf Digest. Golf Magazine* gave it its Number One ranking, and second place went to the short course at Augusta National. The course was originally designed in 1961 by the world renowned golf course architect, Dick Wilson. The Town of Palm Beach purchased the course in 1973 and opened it to the public.

It was redesigned in 2009 by Hall of Fame golfer Raymond Floyd. Today, the course offers 2,572 yards spanning 18 holes, from 81 to 211 yards, and 3 sets of tees on each hole. With the support of the Par 3 Foundation to support junior golfers, this short course has been elevated to world-class status and is consistently named and awarded for its design and play. You'll enjoy breathtaking ocean views as you play through – for less than the price of a movie and popcorn.

Raymond Floyd was a professional golfer until his retirement in 2010. He won over sixty tournaments, including four majors and three senior majors. He took home the green jacket at the 1976 Masters, and he won the 1969 PGA Championships and the 1986 United States Open. He was a member of eight Ryder Cup teams. His focus and determination in the sport has since been shifted to the design and development of golf courses. He creates designs that build upon the natural terrain and influence of the land, while making each hole both challenging and playable. He has completed multiple courses in South Florida, including Grande Oaks, the redesigned filming location of *Caddyshack* (see ch. 97). A popular course for LPGA players and the previous home of the LPGA Pro-Am, the course has hosted several Tour players over the years.

Golfers and non-golfers are welcome to dine in the Club House at the al Fresco Restaurant overlooking the course and the ocean.

Address 2345 S Ocean Boulevard, Palm Beach, FL 33480, +1 (561) 547-0598, www.golfontheocean.com | Getting there From I-95: Take exit 64 and drive east on 10th Avenue North. Turn right on US Highway 1, then left on Lake Avenue and cross bridge onto island. Turn left on S Ocean Boulevard. Course and parking are on the right. | Hours Daily 7:30am–7pm | Tip Hit a full 18-hole course across the Intracoastal at the Lake Worth Golf Club and Beach Club (1 Seventh Avenue North, Lake Worth, www.lakeworthgolfclub.com).

72 — Paramount Theater

Worshipping the classics at church

While the film has stopped rolling at Paramount Theater, the historic picture palace still stands as the Paramount Church, a Christian establishment open to the public. Designed by Joseph Urban in 1926, the Moorish revival and Spanish colonial revival-style building was once the grand theater of the island. Paramount saw the transition to "talkies" from silent pictures and hosted many a who's-who in its heyday. The "Diamond Horseshoe," so nicknamed by *The New York Times* for its 26 raised balcony boxes that curved around the theater, sold out during the 13-week seasons. After decades of films and live performances by greats like Barbra Streisand, the theater closed in 1980 with a showing of *Coal Miner's Daughter.*

Urban was an Austrian-born architect and designer, who is credited as one of the originators of the American art deco style. His prolific career began at the tender age of 19 with his first commission in Cairo, Egypt. His point of view was highly regarded for its innovation, vibrancy, and theatrical ornamentation. This could be seen in the floor to ceiling murals that graced the Paramount, depicting fish swimming through seaweed in hues of blue, green, and gold. Some of his most famous production designs include scenes for the Ziegfeld Follies on Broadway and the Metropolitan Opera. Urban died in 1933 at the age of 61. While many of his properties have since been demolished, Palm Beach is home to a handful of his designs.

In 1994, Paramount Church was founded and placed its sanctuary in the location of the original stage, screen, and orchestra pit. In the early 2000s, residents requested that the church show classic movies for the community. The showing of *Beau Geste*, coincidentally also the first picture ever shown at the theater, was a success, and the movies became a permanent programming feature, bringing back Paramount's original glory.

Address 139 N County Road, Palm Beach, FL 33480, +1 (561) 835-0200, www.paramountchurchpb.com, paramountchurchpb@gmail.com | Getting there From I-95: Take exit 71 and drive east on Palm Beach Lakes Boulevard for about 2.5 miles. Turn right on US Highway 1, then left on North Quadrille Boulevard. Cross the bridge onto the island, and go left on North County Road. Theater is on the right. | Hours Sun 10:30am–1pm; see website for movie schedule | Tip Drive by the 85,000-square-foot Bath and Tennis Club to experience more of Joseph Urban's design aesthetic (1170 S Ocean Boulevard, Palm Beach, www.bath and tennis club.com).

73 Railcar 91 at Whitehall

Travel back in time at Flagler Museum

Beyond the wrought iron gates stands the iconic Henry Morrison Flagler Museum. Situated along the eastern bank of Lake Worth the sprawling estate known as Whitehall was 100,000 square feet and housed over 75 rooms when it was built in 1902. Henry Flagler was a founding partner of Standard Oil with John D. Rockefeller in the late-1800s. After a visit to St. Augustine, Flagler recognized the potential for tourism in Florida. He developed the Florida East Coast Railway system, which led him to Palm Beach, Miami, and eventually Key West. Along the way he created a hotel empire including The Hotel Royal Poinciana and the Palm Beach Inn, later renamed The Breakers (see ch. 39).

Flagler's private Railcar No. 91, part of the first train to pull into Key West after crossing the Over-Seas Railroad, sits restored in the Flagler Kenan Pavilion. The green train car features meticulous wood details, tasseled window coverings, and luxurious interior appointments. It was heralded as a "palace on wheels."

This stunning National Historic Landmark building was a wedding gift from Henry Flagler to his third wife, Mary Lily Kenan, and served as their winter home. Designed by John Carrere and Thomas Hastings, of New York Library fame, the residence reflects the Gilded Age with its statement façade, grand double staircase, soaring great rooms, ornate murals, extensive use of marble, and nod to the temples of Apollo. Pottier & Stymus of New York were tasked with interior decorating and chose furnishings reflective of French kings and the Italian Renaissance. The building materials and methods, and the use of electricity and modern fixtures made this home technologically advanced for its time.

Sadly at the age of 83, Henry Flagler fell down a flight of stairs at the home and subsequently died from injuries sustained. The museum is open to the public and offers an array of programs and events.

Address 1 Whitehall Way, Palm Beach, FL 33480, +1 (561) 655-2833, www.flaglermuseum.us | Getting there From I-95: Take exit 70 and drive east on Okeechobee Boulevard about three miles. Cross the bridge over the Intracoastal Waterway onto Royal Palm Way. Left onto Cocoanut Row. Continue North about 0.5 mile to parking area on the left. | Hours Tue–Sat 10am–5pm, Sun noon–5pm | Tip Don't miss the Kapok Tree in the gardens at the adjacent Royal Poinciana Chapel, a favorite of locals and tourists for photographs (60 Cocoanut Row, Palm Beach, www.royalpoincianachapel.org).

74 Rapids Water Park

Slide through the Brain Drain

Spanning 30 acres with over 40 slides and attractions, Rapids Water Park offers fun in the sun for everyone. Founded in 1979, the water park has been a seasonal retreat from the summer's high temperatures for decades. Expanding beyond its initial footprint, the park has seen many changes over the years, with the slides growing taller and faster and the additions of wave pools, surf simulators, and interactive obstacle courses making Rapids the largest water park in South Florida. Due to the bright colors and activity, the park has also proven to be a popular location for pop culture filming.

In 1997, a young Johnny Depp and Al Pacino filmed at Rapids for the mafia classic *Donnie Brasco*. Depp and Michael Madsen are shown making their way down the original "Old Yellar" open air slides of the park. In 2000, Miami-born rapper Trina filmed the music video for Hot 100 single "Pull Over," tubing through the quarter-mile long lazy river attraction. Fifteen years later, the band *Chvrches* revisited the park for a more goth-inspired video for "Empty Threat." They circled through some of the newer slides, like the funneling Big Thunder.

The water park has hosted many celebrities, including professional racing driver Danica Patrick, and provided a backdrop in commercials for brands like New Balance. But not all have proven to be welcome. When the cast of MTV's *Jersey Shore* moved filming to Miami, their request for access to film was denied due to their penchant for drama.

Rapids features mild to wild rides with height requirements, playful attractions, and calmer pools geared towards small children. You can enjoy a meal or snack at Big Surf or Pelican Bay cafes, and if you're over 21, cool off with a cocktail from one of the tiki bars. Cabanas and picnic pavilions are available as well. Whatever the activity, do not forget to lather on the sunscreen.

Address 6566 N Military Trail, Riviera Beach, FL 33407, +1 (561) 848-6272, www.rapidswaterpark.com, info@RapidsWaterPark.com | Getting there From I-95: Take exit 76 and drive east on Blue Heron Boulevard. Take N Military Trail to Port West Boulevard. Park and parking on the left. | Hours See website for seasonal schedule | Tip For more waterpark fun, visit Calypso Bay Water Park (151 Lamstein Lane, Royal Palm Beach, www.calypsobaywaterpark.com).

75 Raptis Rare Books

Printed, bound, and preserved through time

Raptis Rare Books is not your average bookstore. It specializes in hard-to-find books, including first editions, signed and inscribed books, and other antiquarian gems. When you walk into the book shop, the experience is reminiscent of entering a formal library, with its rich wooden built-in bookcases, tufted leather wingback chairs, marble busts, and rare titles enclosed in glass displays. Founders Matthew and Adrienne Raptis treat books as pieces of created and recorded history, and they connect those who share their passion with the antiquarian delights they covet.

At any given time, the catalog of titles available to discerning collectors includes first editions of sought-after works like Walt Whitman's *Leaves of Grass,* F. Scott Fitzgerald's *The Great Gatsby*, and A. A. Milne's *Winnie the Pooh*. Historically important writings, like the 1788 calfskin-bound *The Federalist: A Collection of Essays*, can warrant price tags upwards of $250,000. Complete book sets, like the *James Bond* series by Ian Fleming, are also available.

Beyond the bookshelf, Raptis offers collectibles with framed original signed letters of significance and autographs of prominent figures, like Abraham Lincoln and Frederick Douglass. Items are valued based on several factors, such as rarity and condition. Covering hundreds of years across many topics and origins, the store is much like a museum, only the artifacts are for sale.

Raptis works with individuals and institutions to acquire exceptional writings. Whether you wish to add to the prestige of a private or public library or to present the perfect gift, the Raptis team scours the world for titles across all genres. The Worth Avenue storefront entices window shoppers with the spines and covers of some of the most unique printings on the literary market. You can also go there to enjoy temporary exhibits of notable memorabilia, lecture series, and other literary events.

Address 226 Worth Avenue, Palm Beach, FL 33480, +1 (561) 508-3479, www.raptisrarebooks.com, mail@raptisrarebooks.com | **Getting there** From I-95: Take exit 70 and drive east on Okeechobee Boulevard. Continue straight onto Royal Park Bridge, which turns into Royal Palm Way. Turn right onto S County Road, then right onto Worth Avenue. The destination is on the left. Street parking available. | **Hours** Mon–Sat 10am–6pm | **Tip** Visit Murder on the Beach Mystery Bookstore for a specialized selection of mystery, thrillers, and suspense novels (104 W Atlantic Avenue, Delray Beach, https://murderonthebeach.com).

76_Rhythm & Hues
Coloring outside the lines

Founded in 2015, Rhythm & Hues Children's Art and Music Center opened with the goal of providing families with a creative outlet for children of all ages. Offering a range of classes, workshops, and events geared towards expression through art and music, the center encourages participants as young as one month to explore their creativity. Started by Courtney Palacios, the vision was largely inspired by her time as a mother and nanny.

Rhythm & Hues strives to make art accessible to everyone, regardless of talent, age, or time constraints, and the programming caters to working families and their little ones. You can sign up for classes for children from three months to twelve years old. Parents can choose from family classes with their kids, group workshops, camps, or private lessons, with flexible hours and enrollment options to suit different needs. Music instruction includes the exploration of instruments from the ukulele to the piano, along with voice lessons. Art classes vary from blank canvas drawing to inspired learning.

Rhythm and Hues' business design has an overall goal of expansion to new locations, with the hope of revitalizing historic properties, building community, and keeping the arts alive in neighborhoods throughout the country. The center transformed their historic 1960 building in the Dixie Corridor into an eco-friendly studio, with a radiating rainbow mural facing the heavily trafficked thoroughfare.

Their mission to "joyfully express creativity" radiates from their space into the surrounding community. Their annual Rainbowpalooza, or "Festival of Kindness," fills areas of West Palm Beach with rainbows and brings families together to celebrate art and music through interactive activities, art stations, live music, and games. The Festival's proceeds go to a spotlighted childrens' charity, such as The Cotton Bottom Diaper Bank.

Address 5016 S Dixie Highway, West Palm Beach, FL 33405, +1 (561) 216-1027, www.rhythmandhues.com | Getting there From I-95: Take exit 68 and drive east on Southern Boulevard. Turn right onto US Highway 1 South. Destination and parking is on the left. | Hours See website for event schedule | Tip Immerse yourself in art and paint at artNEST (2275 S Federal Highway, Unit 340, Delray Beach, www.artneststudios.com).

77 _ Richard & Pat Johnson Museum

Palm Beach history at the courthouse

For over a decade, The Richard & Pat Johnson Museum has been providing access to the history of Palm Beach. It is located within the 1916 Palm Beach County Courthouse, which also serves as the home to the Historical Society of Palm Beach County. Featuring state-of-the-art, interactive exhibits, this 3,000-square-foot space encompasses the history and culture that developed the area into what it is today. Guests can read up on important people and places like those of the Seminole tribe, and view authentic relics and replicas, such as a "Palm Beach Coach" pedaled wicker seat used for transportation by the wealthy.

Richard Johnson was born in West Palm Beach in 1930. He married Patsy "Pat" Seaton in 1951. A well-respected member of the county, Richard was known for his philanthropy and involvement in the community. He served on the board of the Palm Beach Civic Association, and, together with Pat, donated $1.25 million to help in the building of their namesake museum. Richard worked in insurance and real estate, founding and managing several local companies. During his life he served various boards, including Norton Museum of Art (see ch. 66) and Palm Beach Atlantic University. He received several awards for his contributions before his death in 2012 at age 82.

The Main Gallery features topics that change annually from shipwrecks to baseball, while short-term exhibits like those on women's equality and posters of Florida films circulate through the historic Courtroom. The People Gallery and Places Gallery are permanent and pay homage to the natives and pioneers who have helped shape Palm Beach County over the decades, and the early dwellings and natural elements of the area. Visitors can see a life-size replica of the famed barefoot mailman, who delivered the mail without a clear roadway up and down the 70-mile route along the coast (see ch. 31).

Address 300 N Dixie Highway, West Palm Beach, FL 33401, +1 (561) 832-4164, www.hspbc.org | Getting there From I-95: Take exit 71 and drive east on Palm Beach Lakes Boulevard. Turn right on N Australian Avenue. Then left on 1st Street, and left on N Dixie Highway. Museum is on the right with street parking and garage parking available nearby. | Hours Mon–Fri 10am–5pm, Sat 10am–4pm | Tip Few know about the six 1940 murals depicting *The Legend of James Edward Hamilton, Mail Carrier* in the West Palm Beach Post Office (3200 Summit Boulevard, West Palm Beach).

78 Riddle House

Enter if you dare at Yesteryear Village

The Riddle House, or "Painted Lady," was originally built as a funeral parlor in 1905 adjacent to Woodlawn Cemetery (see ch. 31). The building became known as the "Gatekeeper's Cottage" after a string of crimes plagued the cemetery, forcing on-site security measures. It is believed an employee named Buck was killed there during a violent altercation.

Karl Riddle, a city manager and cemetery supervisor, then took up residence in the home and became its namesake. But his peaceful stay was interrupted when an employee hanged himself in the attic. After that death, Riddle began experiencing incidents, like sounds on the stairs and sightings in the attic. Over time, visitors refused to enter the house, as they could feel a presence touching them. The family relocated.

These strange occurrences rendered the property highly undesirable. So the structure was set to be demolished, until John Riddle, Karl's nephew, moved to transport it to Yesteryear Village, as he was a chairman of the living history park. The process was daunting, with reported instances of tools moving and windows breaking. The unveiling in its new home even caused a stir as a long-deceased couple, later found in a picture in the house, were seen at the event. The house has since become the focal point of investigations, television shows, and ghost tours and is considered one of the most active haunts in South Florida. Visitors report seeing the attic light inexplicably shining, shadows of a figure in the window, and eerie sounds emanating from the vacant home.

The nine-acre Yesteryear Village is accessible to the public and features a collection of buildings and homes, originals and replicas, representing the late 1800s and early 1900s. Tour a vintage school, farm, blacksmith shop, general store, and the only big band museum in the country, the Sally Bennett Big Band Hall of Fame Museum.

Address 9067 Southern Boulevard, West Palm Beach, FL 33411, +1 (561) 793-0333, www.southfloridafair.com | Getting there From I-95: Take exit 68 and drive west on Southern Boulevard about seven miles. Fairgrounds and parking lots are on the right. | Hours Thu – Sat 10am – 4pm | Tip Don't miss the Annual South Florida Fair held every January on the fairgrounds (9067 Southern Boulevard, West Palm Beach).

79 Rolls-Royce under the Sea
Buried treasure in the Palm Beach Triangle

Eighty feet below the surface of the Atlantic Ocean rests a two-tone 1967 Silver Shadow. In 1985, Greg Hauptner, a local hairdresser to the rich and famous, stood dressed in a Yves Saint Laurent dinner jacket and sipped champagne while he watched his limited edition Rolls-Royce sink to the bottom of the ocean. While some were furious at his decision, others praised his vehicular sacrifice, as it was his way of helping draw attention to the need for artificial reefs.

The exploration of life under the ocean is a beloved pastime of Palm Beach. Just 10 minutes from the Palm Beach Inlet rests "The Corridor" with an impressive number of wrecks turned reefs. Boynton Beach is home to the Lofthus Shipwreck, a Norwegian iron-hulled sailing vessel that met its watery fate just before the turn of the twentieth century. The vessel, originally known as the *Cashmere*, measured over 200 feet long. After its 1898 wreck, the crew was rescued and the remnants including 800,000 feet of lumber were sold. However, when it was discovered the lumber was more valuable than the now sunken vessel and could be salvaged, the hull was dynamited creating a larger wreckage area of almost 300 feet with several areas to explore. Heading south to Delray Beach, divers will discover the S.S. *Inchulva* or "Delray Wreck." Located about 500 feet from the shoreline, the ship sank during a 1903 hurricane. While much of the almost 400-foot wreck has been covered by sand or washed away, this location still provides great snorkeling and scuba opportunities, especially in the vicinity of the boiler.

Hauptner's Rolls-Royce is located in a dive area known as "The Triangle" that sits about a mile from the Palm Beach Inlet. Divers can also swim the surrounding 150-foot *Eidsvag*, or *Owens*, freighter wreckage and *Murphy's Barge*. Over the years, the car has deteriorated and been pillaged, the hood ornament being stolen; however, an insurance claim has yet to be filed.

Address The Triangle, Atlantic Ocean, www.thepalmbeaches.com | Getting there All dive sites are accessible by boat, privately or chartered through a diving service | Hours Unrestricted | Tip Book a dive trip with Pura Vida Divers for guided charters to underwater sites (2513 Beach Court, Singer Island, www.puravidadivers.com).

80 Royal Palm Way
Travel through the namesake palms

Just over the Royal Park Bridge, the road becomes flanked with rows of towering royal palm trees. They serve as the perfect welcoming entryway into the alluring Town of Palm Beach, providing a canopy of fronds and the inspiration for the island's name. The abundance of palms dates back to a 1878 boating accident, in which a ship set sail from Trinidad to Spain, only to land in South Florida.

Over a century ago, Spanish brigantine *La Providenia* began its journey to Cadiz by way of Havana. Stocked with cargo, including Cuban rum and cigars, the 175-ton ship ran aground on the island then known as Lake Worth Region. Believing they were in Mexico, the drunken crew brought ashore the ship's load of 20,000 coconuts. They drank and mingled by the beach with the locals until being picked up a few weeks later by a passing boat. Local William Lanehart claimed the *Providencia* wreck from the insurance company. After selling some of the coconuts, he planted many in the hopes of creating groves for farming. The name "Palm City" was taken by a settlement to the North, so the community decided on "Palm Beach."

The town wouldn't incorporate until 1911, in a successful attempt to avoid annexation by nearby West Palm Beach. Lanehart and his friend, Hiram Hammon, filed two of the first homesteads in the area, which included the land now occupied by Worth Avenue. When Hammon's homestead was sold, the US Department of Interior deemed it the most valuable claim filed to date.

The *Providencia* is credited with creating the lush tropical feel that was so appealing to pioneers and tourists, and has become a popular moniker for local products like Providencia Rum and tourism awards. Enjoy the result of its cargo by hopping in a convertible with the top down or opening the sunroof and rolling down the windows to take in the sun's rays through the flicker of the palms.

Address Royal Palm Way, Palm Beach, FL 33480 | **Getting there** From I-95: Take exit 70 and drive east on Okeechobee Boulevard. Take the Royal Park Bridge onto the island. The road will become Royal Palm Way. | **Hours** Unrestricted | **Tip** Walk or drive the palm tree-lined Royal Poinciana Way just over the North Bridge on the island.

81 Science on a Sphere

Full circle at South Florida Science Museum

Founded by the Junior League of the Palm Beaches, the South Florida Science Museum and Aquarium opened in 1961 to create a learning environment for natural science and history. Over the years, the exhibits and focus expanded to include a planetarium, aquarium, science trail, and putt-putt conservation golf course designed by Gary Nicklaus and Jim Fazio.

The Science Museum hosts an array of permanent and traveling exhibits throughout the year and is home to the famed Science on a Sphere (SOS). Developed by NOAA researchers, the SOS is a room-sized, 200-pound, fiberglass, spherical global display system that uses computers and projectors to display planetary data in 3D. The result is a six-foot-diameter animation that can be used as an educational tool to help illustrate Earth System science through imaging. You can visualize atmospheric storms, climate change, ocean temperatures, and animal migration patterns around the globe. The SOS was funded by the Quantum Foundation, which has been a longtime supporter of the museum and exhibit developments, including the $2.5-million "Journey Through the Human Brain."

Continuing through the museum, you'll enter an interactive area, with displays like the Hurricane Simulator that allow you to step into science and experience hurricane force winds up to 100mph. The museum connects to the Aquariums of the Atlantic, which features over 8,000 gallons filled with aquatic life, where guests can view Florida fish, reefs, and ecosystems. You also have the option to pop into the center of an aquarium for up close and personal viewing. The first planetarium in Palm Beach County, the Dekelboum Planetarium is open daily and offers a monthly laser light show combining themed music with an awe-inspiring visual light performance. The immersive nature of the museum is geared towards opening the minds of its visitors to science.

Address 4801 Dreher Trail North, West Palm Beach, FL 33405, +1 (561) 832-1988, www.sfsciencecenter.org | Getting there From I-95: Take exit 68 and drive east for about 0.5 mile. Turn right on Parker Avenue. Turn right on Summit Boulevard. Turn right on Dreher Trail N. Museum is on the left. | Hours Mon – Fri 9am – 5pm, Sat & Sun 10am – 6pm | Tip Make your way into the surrounding Dreher Park for fishing, wildlife viewing and family fun (100 Southern Boulevard, West Palm Beach, www.wpb.org).

82 Serenity Garden

Bring tiers to your eyes at tea time

Step through the front door of this historic cottage, complete with white picket fence and garden, into an eclectic arrangement of tables and settings adorned with fine china, cloth napkins, teacups, and flowers. Welcome to Serenity Garden. Each room of the house is now a dining room, layered with oriental rugs, lace tablecloths, floral place settings, and classic trinkets, transporting sippers to a time of fanciful meals and social engagements. The atmosphere is relaxed but sophisticated, with a whimsically chic aesthetic. Guests can partake in lunch, afternoon tea, or simply purchase their favorite loose-leaf teas to savor at home.

Once a mid-afternoon social gathering, the concept of afternoon tea originated in England in the 1840s. Also referred to as "low tea," due to the rich being able to lounge in low chairs, the concept was born when Anna the Duchess of Bedford wanted a small bite between breakfast and dinner. A snack she began taking privately in her room grew as she invited friends to join and eventually planned a more formal gathering in the drawing room. The high society of London took quickly to this newly created mealtime, and it has since become a way for people to relive the days of British aristocracy.

Be seated for afternoon tea, featuring homemade scones with clotted cream and preserves, finger sandwiches, petit fours, and a selection of teas for your own personal teapot. A lunch menu is available to order à la carte. For a more extravagant experience, order the Royal Tea and indulge in a glass of champagne before tea service begins. With 50 loose-leaf organic teas ranging from white, green, and black on the menu, there is surely something for every taste. Tea isn't just for grownups, as little ones can enjoy an adorable Tot Tea platter with sandwiches, snacks, and desserts served with a lemonade or chocolate milk in lieu of tea.

Address 316 Vallette Way, West Palm Beach, FL 33401, +1 (561) 655-3911, www.serenitygardentea.com | Getting there From I-95: Take exit 70 and drive east on Okeechobee Boulevard. Turn right on US 1 S, then left onto Vallette Way. Tea house is on the right, street parking. | Hours Mon 11:30am–2pm, Tue–Fri 11:30am–5pm, Sat & Sun 11:30am–4pm | Tip Tea lovers can enjoy daily tea with dainty cups and patterned flatware at Teapots and Treasures Café (14137 US Highway 1, Juno Beach, www.teapotsandtreasurescafe.com).

83 __ Sloan's Startling Restroom

Don't forget to lock the door

Some people visit for the ice cream, some just to use the restroom. Either way, Sloan's Ice Cream is a locally beloved creamery that gained international attention with their trick toilet. Stepping through the hot pink front doors, guests are engulfed with bright colors, images of cherubs and treats, multi-colored chandeliers, and all things sweet. The smell of fresh waffle cones fills the shop, while candies and toys catch the eye. But glancing through a large picture window, many are shocked to see they are peering into the restroom. There is even a back table for those enjoying a sundae to dine with a view.

The key to this loo is to read the instructions and make sure you lock the door before you do your business. The bolt lever activates the science behind the nerve-racking window, making it go from clear to fogged for privacy. Between two panels of glass is a layer of liquid crystals suspended by an electric current which is interrupted by the locking of the door and in turn makes the center layer opaque. Those who forget this important step may realize the mistake they've made once exiting to a room of stares and giggles. The risky water closet has been featured on local and national television, including the Travel Channel, and nominated for various best restrooms awards, landing consistently in the top ten in the nation and world.

Those who can't make it to the Rosemary Square location can get in on the fun at one of their other South Florida locations spanning from Doral to West Palm Beach and serving up vibrant treats since 1999. While you're there, enjoy a fresh ice cream cone, a colossal milkshake, inventive sundaes, baked goods, or a chocolate treat. If you dare, order the Tracy's Kitchen Sink, boasting 18 scoops of ice cream, cookies, brownies, whipped cream, and cherries served in what other than a kitchen sink, complete with a faux faucet.

Address 700 S Rosemary Avenue, West Palm Beach, FL 33401, +1 (561) 833-4303, www.sloansicecream.com | Getting there From I-95: Take exit 70 and drive west on Okeechobee Boulevard. Turn left onto S Rosemary Avenue. Sloan's is on the right. Street parking and parking garages available. | Hours Sun–Thu 11am–11pm, Thu–Sat 11am–midnight | Tip Walk down to Clematis Street to visit the original Sloan's flagship and give their restroom a try too (112 S Clematis Street, West Palm Beach, www.sloansicecream.com).

84_ Society of the Four Arts
A living garden classroom

The Society of the Four Arts is a non-profit organization that was founded in 1936 to bring cultural programming to the area. Points of interest include the Gioconda and Joseph King Library, designed by famed architect Maurice Fatio, and the outdoor Philip Hulitar Sculpture Garden Museum featuring works of its namesake, a prominent supporter of the property. The Esther B. O'Keeffe Gallery has a history involving the who's who of Palm Beach. It was originally designed by Addison Mizner (see ch. 50) as the Embassy Club at the request of E. R. Bradley, and John Volk renovated it for its current role.

Maintained by The Garden Club of Palm Beach, the demonstration gardens are reflective of their theme in both architecture and biodiversity. Look for the pinwheel jasmine, bonsai trees, and a koi pond with floating water lilies featured in the Chinese Garden. The Moonlight garden boasts vines and shrubs of white blooms. Over the years, the gardens have taken on new designs and species, but the original gardens were each spearheaded by a founding club member as a way to educate budding home gardeners. Later, landscape architects were retained to create a cohesive master plan, which was used during a major overhaul following a particularly destructive hurricane season. Though the gardens differ in motif, together they showcase the diverse plant varieties that thrive in the balmy climate of Palm Beach.

Beyond its botanicals, the Society of the Four Arts owns over 75,000 books, including the personal library of Addison Mizner, an extensive collection of fine arts, auditorium, children's library, and more. Immerse yourself at this cultural gem, and take advantage of the exhibits, lectures, classes, concerts, and series made available during the season. You can become a member of the libraries directly. Joining the Society of the Four Arts takes a little more time.

Address 100 Four Arts Plaza, Palm Beach, FL 33480, +1 (561) 655-7226, www.fourarts.org | Getting there From I-95: Take exit 70 and drive east on Okeechobee Boulevard. Continue over the Royal Park Bridge. Make the first left turn onto Four Arts Plaza. Gardens are on the left. | Hours Daily 10am–5pm | Tip Visit the living green wall that overlooks Worth Avenue at Esplanade (150 Worth Avenue, Palm Beach).

85 SolarNow Tree

Keeping renewable energy on track at Brightline

Hop aboard the Brightline for high-speed train service from West Palm Beach to Fort Lauderdale and Miami. Connecting three major hubs with more on the way, Brightline brings a level of convenience to the area for commuters and connectivity for tourists and locals. Offering first class-like service with "Select" lounges and seating, riders are treated to complimentary snacks and beverages, plush seating with optional tables, and free WiFi. The trains are powered with clean biodiesel by Florida Power and Light (FPL), creating lower emissions, and upon arrival, passengers pass by a "tree" of solar panels adding to the sustainability factor of the property.

FPL SolarNow solar trees and canopies are innovative structures meant to bring visibility to and educate the community on the clean energy efforts being made locally, while simultaneously providing shade and converting the South Florida sun into usable energy. Headquartered in Juno Beach, NextEra Energy and FPL are major employers of the area, serving as the leading supplier of electric energy in Florida with NextEra recognized as the world's largest producer of wind and solar energy. The Brightline partnership embodies the area's emphasis and focus on renewable energy as the SolarNow program is funded voluntarily through communities and the local population. With diverse locations including Palm Beach International Airport, Joseph R. Russo Athletic Complex, and Palm Beach Zoo, the station marked the hundredth solar tree installation.

The 60,000-square-foot LEED-certified station is steps from the main thoroughfare of downtown, Clematis Street, offering access to dining, shopping, and cultural and entertainment venues. The trains run on a daily schedule with tickets available in-person or through the app, with limited stops to keep on time as they travel at almost 80 miles per hour down the track.

Address 501 Evernia Street, West Palm Beach, FL 33401, +1 (561) 537-8059, www.gobrightline.com, info@GoBrightline.com | Getting there From I-95: Take exit 70 and drive east on Okeechobee Boulevard. Turn left onto S Rosemary Avenue, then right onto Evernia Street. Parking and destination is straight ahead. | Hours See website for hours | Tip Hop aboard the retired Lounge Car 6603 at the Boca Express Train Museum (747 S Dixie Highway, Boca Raton, www.bocahistory.org).

86 — Swank Specialty Produce

Farm to farm table

Swank Specialty Produce is a hydroponic, all-natural farm that harvests over 350 varieties of produce, micro-greens, and wildflowers. Darrin Swank's family had a history in agriculture in Pennsylvania, but Disney World and the rise of the internet is what brought this 20-acre farm to life. A trip to *The Land* exhibit at Epcot inspired Darrin, and subsequent research on real estate in Palm Beach County and farming practices online convinced him to make this concept a reality. Soon, Swank was a popular green market, and customers began requesting lunches on the property.

Swank Table began with a lunch hosted by Chef Dean Max and his team, complete with chef names like Jeremy Ford, Paula DaSilva, and Pushkar Marathe. Before the meal was over, diners were already asking when the next event would be held. One lunch became three, a handful of pop-up tents became a full scale pole barn, and now a lineup of over a dozen on-site dining experiences fills the calendar each year.

Guests are invited to visit the farm, meet the owners, and dine with local chefs for a memorable meal just steps from where the majority of the food was grown. Coffee is prepared in a kettle on the fire, visitors mix and mingle with the chickens and pigs before being seated, and the shade house is open for perusing. Often accompanied by live music and a selection of local artisans, Swank Table dinners invite guests to eat, drink, and dance under the stars. The Master Chef series brings like-minded chefs together from across the country, and the Brunch Series invites you to a morning of breakfast bites and bloody marys.

Swank can still be found at the weekend green markets, selling the leafy greens that made them famous, and other fresh vegetables, herbs, and edible flowers. Their dining series runs through the season, and their produce can be found in local restaurants year round.

Address 14311 N Road, Loxahatchee, FL 33470, +1 (561) 202-5648, www.swankspecialtyproduce.com | **Getting there** From I-95: Take exit 70 and drive west on Okeechobee Boulevard for about 10 miles. Turn right on FL-7N. Turn left on Orange Grove Boulevard. Turn left on 130th Avenue N. Turn right on 40th Street N. Turn right on N Road. Turn right on 145 Avenue. Farm is on the right. | **Hours** See website for event schedule | **Tip** For more farm-side events and locally grown produce, visit Lox Farms (1442 E Road, Loxahatchee, www.loxfarms.com).

87 — Ta-boo's Window Seat

Still the most glamorous seat in town

Ta-boo Restaurant and Bar has stood for decades as the place to see and be seen. Opened in December 1941 by Ted Stone, the bistro quickly became *the* place to go on Palm Beach Island. "A restaurant of international reputation," the once tiki-style bistro was frequented by celebrities like Gary Cooper, Jackie Gleason, Frank Sinatra, and John F. Kennedy, creating a buzz of verified stories and tall tales. One account claims that a morning-after cocktail request by Barbara Hutton led to the obliging bartender creating the Bloody Mary, while another recounts the time during World War II when a German submarine commander snuck ashore to enjoy a cocktail at the legendary bar.

Now owned by Franklyn DeMarco and Nancy Sharigan, the restaurant stands as a Palm Beach society staple. The famous crowd still makes an appearance with patrons like Jimmy Buffet, James Patterson, and Kathy Lee, and reservations are recommended – if not mandatory if you want to dine by the front window for the first seating of the day. The menu is approachable, and the front door is always open, giving Ta-boo a surprisingly inviting atmosphere, despite its reputation for being a haven for the wealthy and well-known. The bar scene is energetic, with live music often making its way to the street over the chatter of the crowd.

Ta-boo celebrated its 75th anniversary, proving its status and outlasting temporary hotspots, while collecting numerous food and wine accolades. The dining rooms have been featured in newspapers, magazines, and tabloids, while generations have enjoyed special occasions as well as a casual bite at their tables. Today, the décor is more refined but maintains a vintage feel and subtle elegance. And while this establishment is considered a "must see and be seen" for tourists, it is a beloved gem to locals and maintains a steady stream of regulars.

Address 221 Worth Avenue, Palm Beach, FL 33480, +1 (561) 835-3500, www.taboorestaurant.com | Getting there From I-95: Take exit 70 and drive east on Okeechobee Boulevard about three miles. Cross the bridge over the Intracoastal Waterway onto Royal Palm Way. Turn right onto S County Road, then right onto Worth Avenue. Restaurant is on the right. Street parking available. | Hours Daily 11:30am–10pm | Tip Walk off your meal with a stroll down the famous Worth Avenue. Visit Kassatly's, the avenue's oldest store since 1923 (250 Worth Avenue, Palm Beach, www.kassatlys.com).

88 Virginia Philip Wine Shop

A sip above the rest at The Royal

In 2002, Virginia Philip became the eleventh woman to earn the Master Sommelier title. Today, her namesake academy hosts an array of events and classes and features a wine and spirits shop. A James Beard nominee for Outstanding Wine & Spirits Professional, Philip is a respected oenophile, who shares her knowledge via her shop, national events and appearances, media, publication contributions, and guided international travel experiences. Her boutique offers hundreds of personally selected labels, creating a standout collection to choose from. Her educational programming in the classroom within the space provides participants with fascinating information and a memorable experience.

Virginia Philip was born in Pennsylvania and raised in Connecticut, and she graduated *magna cum laude* from Johnson & Wales University in Rhode Island in 1989. Her passion and wine studies let her into the hospitality business, where she worked at award-winning resorts. Then she joined the team at The Breakers in Palm Beach, where she has overseen renowned wine lists, blends, and programs. The opening of her wine shop fulfilled a lifelong dream in 2011. In 2015, Philip's *alma mater* presented her with one of the highest honors, an Honorary Doctorate Degree of Oenology.

The wine shop is located in the Royal Poinciana Plaza, designed by famed architect John Volk. The iconic plaza encompasses the lasting glamour and casual elegance of the island with open green space courtyards, black-and-white checkered terrazzo, and a jewel box atmosphere of dining and retail. The Austrian-born, New York-raised designer was given free reign by owner John S. Phipps in an effort to create an enduring aesthetic. With clients like the Vanderbilt, DuPont, Ford, Dodge, and Pulitzer families, Volk was able to deliver on that vision. Over half a century later, the project maintains its architectural appeal.

Address 340 Royal Poinciana Way, Suite 302, Palm Beach, FL 33480, +1 (561) 557-4202, www.virginiaphilipwineshopacademy.com | **Getting there** From I-95: Take exit 70 and drive east on Okeechobee Boulevard about three miles. Cross the bridge over the Intracoastal Waterway onto Royal Palm Way. Turn left on Cocoanut Row. The plaza and parking are on the left. | **Hours** Mon–Sat 10am–7pm, Sun 11am–5pm | **Tip** For families, inquire about Wee Royal programming, with activites including culture, science, and fun for children (340 Royal Poinciana Way, Palm Beach, www.theroyalpoincianaplaza.com).

89 Warehouse District
Breathing life into empty warehouses

The Warehouse District stood not long ago as a group of unremark-able warehouses that served as an industrial business zone at the outskirts of downtown. In late 2015, this collection of structures was purchased with the goal of creating a commingled commu-nity. The redevelopment was anchored by Grandview Public Mar-ket and The Station, creating collaborative shared spaces for local purveyors. Filling in the gap between them came Steam Horse Brewing, District Workspace, and Steel Tie Distillery. The busi-nesses line the abandoned central Seaboard Coast Line train rail, which creates cohesion and provides an outdoor walkway through the district.

The focal point of the redevelopment, Grandview Public Market marked the first food hall concept in the area. It is an epicenter of small businesses expanding into brick and mortar and now features a dozen food vendors and a handful of local boutiques. The main stage of the market is the Loading Dock, an area of congregation where diners enjoy their meals, entrepreneurs work in the fresh air, and programming like salsa night fill the evening sky with music and banter. In the 14,000-square-foot space that offers a multitude of options from coffee and pastries to tacos and pizza, the food vendors are centered around the main bar. Shoppers can wander the novelty stationery store and surf shop, while locals mix, mingle, and work in the Living Room. Each space has its own personality, making this a perfect meeting place for friends, families, co-workers, or private, corporate, and social events.

The District spans three city blocks and over 80,000 square feet of retail and office space. Each venue has a back story of its time since the 1920s and now provides a home for budding concepts that add to the fabric of West Palm Beach. Look for vibrant murals by South Florida artists on many of the interior and exterior walls.

Address 1500 Elizabeth Avenue, West Palm Beach, FL 33401, www.thedistrictwpb.com | **Getting there** From I-95: Take exit 70 and drive east on Okeechobee Boulevard. Turn right on Parker Avenue. Turn right on Caroline Street. Turn left on Clare Avenue. Venue and parking on right. | **Hours** Vary by location | **Tip** Support local small businesses at the West Palm Beach Green Market on the downtown waterfront every Saturday from 9am–1pm October through May (101 S Clematis Street, West Palm Beach, www.wpb.org).

90 WPB Fishing Club
From sportfishing to safeguarding

Exploring downtown, you wouldn't expect to see a metal-roofed, shiplap wood-framed, modern ranch adorned with a large billfish among the towering office buildings. That 1940 clubhouse belongs to the West Palm Beach Fishing Club. Founded in 1934, the club is one of the oldest of its kind, as well as one of the most respected. Its initial purpose was to stimulate the local economy in response to the Great Depression by supporting the charter boat fleet and luring tourists to the area.

Over the decades, the WPB Fishing Club has played a major role in fishing in South Florida by promoting the use of red pennants for catch and release, lobbying for game fish statuses, protecting marine life through ethical fishing and conservation practices, and installing artificial reefs. More recently, their "reef dart" initiative utilizes repurposed concrete poles to create a vertical habitat that is both cost-effective and innovative. The club hosts the annual Silver Sailfish Derby, the oldest continually running billfish release tournament in the world, among other events, and it sponsors educational programs for anglers of all ages. Members have included boat builder John Rybovich, golfer Jack Nicklaus, baseball player Ted Williams, and famed writer Ernest Hemingway. John's wife, Kay Rybovich, was one of four ladies who formed the International Women's Fishing Association in 1955, changing the competitive fishing landscape for women. Former IWFA president Jeanne Stephenson wears a bracelet with charms representing her best catches and awards.

The clubhouse received historical designation with its Dade pine, cypress paneling, and Bahamas shutters. Gamefish hang from the walls and ceilings of the meeting hall, which also features an exhibit space and a display of club records. The club boasts a membership of over 1,000 youth, men, and women, including several members since birth.

Address 201 5th Street, West Palm Beach, FL 33401, +1 (561) 832-6780, www.westpalmbeachfishingclub.org, wpbfc@westpalmbeachfishingclub.org | **Getting there** From I-95: Take exit 71 and drive east on Palm Beach Lakes Boulevard. Turn right on N Flagler Drive. Turn right on 5th Street. Club and parking on the right. | **Hours** Unrestricted from the outside or by appointment | **Tip** Take a stroll down Flagler Drive and walk out onto the public Clematis and Fern docks of West Palm Beach to enjoy the views of Lake Worth Lagoon (401 Clematis Street, West Palm Beach, www.wpb.org).

91 Arthur R. Marshall Park

Entrance to the glades

Arthur R. Marshall Loxahatchee National Wildlife Refuge is the only entry point to the Everglades in Palm Beach County. Established in 1951 under the Migratory Bird Conservation Act, the refuge offers visitors a variety of activities, from hunting and fishing, to wildlife tours and photography. The almost 150,000-acre area creates a 225-square-mile buffer between the development of South Florida and the Everglades.

Arthur R. Marshall moved to Palm Beach County in 1925 at the age of six. His interest in the water began with fishing, boating, and swimming in the South Florida waterways. After serving in World War II, he returned to Florida, where he studied biology and later marine science. He spent most of his life working and studying various marine creatures from snook to shrimp, and the intricacies of ecosystems. He delved into the impact of fishing, farming, and development on water quality and ecological health. His interest and knowledge led to various papers, plans for preservation, and conservation efforts. In 1984, the Florida Wildlife Federation named Marshall "Conservationist of the Decade." He died the following year. Because of his commitment to the environment, his name is memorialized on the refuge, an endowment at the University of Florida, and a local conservation foundation.

Everglades National Park as a whole features over one million acres of wetland preserves. The iconic grassy ecosystem is a protective home to various wildlife species, including the keystone American alligator. The Loxahatchee Wildlife Refuge offers public access in the Headquarters area. Visitors are invited to explore the looping boardwalk Cypress Trail or Marsh Trail along the dike system. Due to its expansive water and swamplands, much of the park is accessible only by airboat, kayak, or canoe. Relax and enjoy the serene views, but don't forget insect repellent.

Address 10216 Lee Road, Boynton Beach, FL 33473 +1 (561) 734-8303, www.fws.gov | Getting there From I-95: Take exit 57 and drive west on Boynton Beach Boulevard for about eight miles. Turn left on US 441, then right on Lee Road. Park entrance and parking on the right. | Hours Daily 5am–10pm | Tip Experience the splendor of the Everglades from an airboat perch. Glide along the waterways through rivers of grass, while keeping an eye out for alligators and wildlife on a guided tour. It's not just for tourists (15490 Loxahatchee Road, Parkland, www.evergladesairboattours.com).

92 Artists Alley

Discover local talent in Pineapple Grove

To find the Pineapple Grove Art District, simply look for the massive, block-long pineapple mural pointing you in the direction of the vibrant bromeliad archway. The first mural by local artist Anita Lovitt, the international symbol for hospitality dances down the block, welcoming pedestrians, cyclists, and motorists in eclectic colors signifying the diversity of the area. A haven for emerging talent, the grove is home to colonies of artists showcasing their work through studios, classrooms, and galleries.

Artists Alley is a collection of independent, arts-focused warehouses that tie together a collaborative community of local creators. A hub for an array of art mediums, Arts Warehouse is an incubator providing guidance on an international level with educational programming and gallery exhibitions. Small private studios provide space for creatives to hone their crafts, with talents like fashion designer Amanda Perna of *Project Runway* fame occupying suites. The Arts Garage has created a not-for-profit community that cultivates a dynamic and wide-ranging programming calendar, displaying art forms, including fine art, award winning musical acts, and drag shows. Visit the Grassroots Gallery here, which showcases emerging local talent and provides an opportunity for artists to gain exposure and entry into the art world. The gallery is open and free to the public, and a large percentage of sale proceeds go directly to the artists.

You'll appreciate the diverse talent to be found in Pineapple Grove and the lively vibe is complemented by local restaurants, bars, and businesses that create an active social scene in the neighborhood. The arts district folds seamlessly into the fabric of Delray Beach, which is home to The Delray Affair, one of the largest arts and crafts festivals in the Southeast US that spans over a dozen city blocks during its annual run in April.

Address 94 NE 2nd Avenue, Delray Beach, FL 33444, +1 (561) 450-6357, www.artsgarage.org | Getting there From I-95: Take exit 52 and drive east on Atlantic Avenue. Turn left onto NW 1st Avenue, then right onto NW 1st Street. Turn right onto NE 2nd Avenue. Garage and parking are on the right. | Hours See website for event schedules | Tip Across Atlantic Avenue from Pineapple Grove, visit Proper Ice Cream for inventive flavors, like strawberry biscuits and cream or blood orange sorbet (75 SE 4th Avenue, Delray Beach, www.propericecream.com).

93 Bedner Farms U-Pick
Farm to basket shopping

Bedner's Farm Fresh Market is a family owned and operated farmer's market located on their second generation, 80-acre farm. Shoppers are greeted with aisles of fresh, colorful produce direct from the farm, alongside sun-soaked flowers, curated wines, and unique snacks. An interactive element to the property is the "U-Pick" program, where visitors gather their own strawberries, peppers, cucumbers, and tomatoes, depending on the season. Sunflower season runs in the spring from February to May.

In the 1950s, Arthur Bedner, a transplant from Pennsylvania, moved to South Florida to pursue his farming dreams. With only 20 dollars in his pocket and his new bride Henrietta by his side, he forged his way, starting the farm in 1960. Nurturing an array of crops and working with other farmers to best utilize the land, Arthur grew his agricultural vision into a thriving business that he eventually handed off to his sons. With fresh eyes on its future, Steve, Bruce, and Charlie expanded the operations. The property features a 9,800-square-foot barn-style market where much of the stock comes from the surrounding acreage. The farm focuses on sustainable practices and strives to be a leader in the movement. The Bedner family name can also be seen at their local retail shops in the area. Arthur passed away in 2007 at the age of 85, but his farming legacy is still strong over a decade later.

Bedner's Farm offers admission-free entry. Visitors can shop the market, book a field trip to tour the farm atop a tractor tram, or fill their baskets with fresh fruits and vegetables straight off the vine. During the holidays, the market offers all-natural turkeys and freshly baked pies, while the Pumpkin Patch provides a backdrop for their Fall Festival. Families come for the special events, which often include petting zoos, face painting, and a corn maze. Go for the delicious, fresh produce. Stay for the fun.

Address 10066 Lee Road, Boynton Beach, FL 33473 +1 (561) 733-5490, www.bedners.com |
Getting there From I-95: Take exit 57 and drive west on Boynton Beach Road for about
eight miles. Turn left on US-441S, then right on Lee Road. Market and parking on the
right. | Hours Mon–Sat 9am–6pm, Sun 10am–5pm | Tip Experience the farm in down-
town Delray Beach at Bedner's Farm Fresh Market (381 NE 3rd Avenue, Delray Beach,
www.bedner's.com).

94 Benny's on the Beach
A meal above the Atlantic

Situated on the William O. Lockhart Municipal Pier is Benny's on the Beach, a Lake Worth landmark serving breakfast, lunch, and dinner daily. Since 1986, diners have literally looked down on the Atlantic from above the sands of Lake Worth Beach, while enjoying American fare and seafood – from pancakes to paella. The only full-service restaurant on a pier from Dania Beach up to Cocoa Beach, Benny's proudly serves "Beach Cuisine," using fresh ingredients to create food meant to be enjoyed from a perch atop the ocean.

The name "Benny's" is a mystery, even to its current owners. It is rumored that the name was chosen as a nod to the nickname for Eggs Benedict, as the restaurant was originally a breakfast joint. In 2013, the Lipton father and son team purchased the restaurant in partnership with world-class celebrity chef Jeremy Hanlon. Together, their team worked to elevate the menu and expanded to three meals a day. Guests can now dive into shrimp and grits for breakfast, Crowd Favorite Tacos for lunch, or their famous Seafood Bake for dinner. The unbeatable views, combined with coconut-bound cocktails and eclectic menu, have lured celebrities like Jon Bon Jovi, Serena Williams, Adam Richman, and Daniel Tosh. Daily live entertainment and beach-clad people watching add to the atmosphere.

Benny's is located at the entrance of the city's public pier, renamed in 2003 in honor of the late pier master Lockhart, who was also heavily involved in the community and a local activist. You are invited to explore the surrounding beach or stroll the pier (for a small fee). Pier fishing is also available for a few dollars more. Diners can be seen sipping daiquiris from hollowed pineapples, while playing trivia or awaiting their turn at karaoke, depending on the day. Benny's has found a philosophy that resonates with locals and tourists alike: "Live like every day is a vacation."

Address 10 S Ocean Boulevard, Lake Worth, FL 33460, +1 (561) 582-9001, www.bennysonthebeach.com, info@bennysonthebeach.com · Getting there: From I-95: Take exit 64 and drive east on 10th Avenue N. Turn right on US Highway 1, then left on Lake Avenue, and continue straight over the bridge. Turn right on A1A. Lake Worth Beach Park and parking are on the left. · Hours: Daily 7am–9pm · Tip: Visit the nearby Lake Worth Casino. The name pays homage to its 1920s past, but the beachside complex for dining, shopping, and entertainment does not feature a casino (10 S Ocean Boulevard, Lake Worth Beach, www.lakeworthbeachfl.gov/casino-and-beach-complex).

95 The Blue Anchor

Pints and spirits at a spooky good bar

While The Blue Anchor may sit on sunny Atlantic Avenue, its history dates back to the 19th century and another continent altogether. The original pub was built in the mid-1800s, not in South Florida, but on Chancery Lane in London, England, where it served bangers and mash and during the days – and nights – of Jack the Ripper. The owners tore down the establishment, but the façade and interior were spared and shipped across the Atlantic Ocean to New York, where they stayed in storage until fate brought them to Delray Beach.

The Blue Anchor made its way to the States thanks to a man named Lee Harrison. A reporter for the *National Enquirer*, he decided to rebuild the watering hole when another fellow Englishman complained of not having a good British pub in the area. What better pub to bring than one that had served Winston Churchill in its original glory? While the pieces made their way, with them came their history. This includes the haunting of Bertha Starkey, a British woman who was stabbed to death by her husband, who discovered her with another man at the bar. It is believed she was murdered at ten o'clock at night, which became her witching hour, especially in the snug section. To keep her at bay, the owners ring the bar's ship bell each night at that time so patrons can continue to enjoy their pints of beer and fish and chips without her interrupting.

In 2017, Mark and Peggy Snyder purchased the bar and its phantom tenant, who immediately made her presence known by launching a decorative relic from the walls. The establishment has been featured on various supernatural series and had its paranormal activity verified. Bertha's ghost hasn't affected business, however, as The Blue Anchor is the longest consecutively running restaurant in Delray Beach. The British paraphernalia, the cheering football fans, and the hand-pump beer taps keep clients coming back.

Address 804 E Atlantic Avenue, Delray Beach, FL 33483, +1 (561) 272-7272, www.theblueanchorpub.com | Getting there From I-95: Take exit 52 and drive east on Atlantic Avenue for about 1.5 miles. Pub is on the right with parking behind. | Hours Mon–Fri 11:30–2am, Sat & Sun 11–2am | Tip Continue east on Atlantic Avenue to visit New England in Delray Beach at Boston's on the Beach (40 S Ocean Boulevard, Delray Beach, www.bostonsonthebeach.com).

96 Bodies in the Gulfstream
A chilling tale along Boynton Beach

Taking a visit to Ocean Inlet Park, you are greeted with sparkling waters, boats making their way through the Boynton Beach Inlet, and fisherman casting off. But below the surface of the ocean lies the resting place of one of the most complicated criminal cases in county history.

On June 15, 1955 Judge Curtis E. Chillingworth opened his Manalapan home to a two-man ambush, and he and wife Marjorie were kidnapped. Evidence pointed to foul play, but no arrests. Years later, the case finally came together when Floyd "Lucky" Holsapfel, one of the assailants, told the story about how he and Bobby Lincoln were paid $2,500 to assassinate the judge.

Both defendants testified that they "did it for Joe," referring to a fellow judge, Joseph A. Peel. As details of their terrifying evening emerged, the community learned that the Chillingsworths had been thrown into the ocean with weights to anchor their watery demise. Their killers would tell how they reaffirmed their love for one another before the assassins threw Marjorie overboard to the old adage, "Ladies first!"

The motive was greed. Judge Peel needed to protect his station so as to secure payoffs from gamblers and moonshiners. Chillingsworth had uncovered and vowed to expose Peel's corruption, and for that, he paid with his life. Holzapfel was sentenced to life in prison, where he died in 1996. Lincoln was given immunity in exchange for his testimony and passed away a free man in 2004. Peel, the mastermind, served 21 years in federal prison before he was released on parole due to his battle with terminal cancer. In 1982, he died, just nine days after his release after admitting his guilt on his deathbed.

So think of Curtis and Marjorie as you stroll along Manalapan's beach. Knowing their story may feel a bit eerie, but the sand and the landscape make it a lovely spot to enjoy the sunshine.

Address 6990 N Ocean Boulevard, Boynton Beach, FL 33435, +1 (561) 966-6600, discover.pbcgov.org | Getting there From I-95: Take exit 57 and drive east on Boynton Beach Boulevard. Turn right on US Highway 1, then left on E Ocean Avenue. Turn left on N Ocean Boulevard, then left on Sea Lake Drive. Park and parking are on the right. | Hours Daily dawn–dusk | Tip Visit the nearby Dinosaur Playground for fun in the sun with friends and family (65 Sea Lake Drive #1, Ocean Ridge).

97 — Caddyshack Was Here
No gophers allowed

The Boca Raton Resort is the location where many of the interior shots, including the dining and dancing scene, were filmed for the cult classic movie *Caddyshack*. The movie's "Bushwood" golf course itself is located just south at Grand Oaks, formerly Rolling Hills, in Davie. Rolling Hills Country Club played host to a number of notables, including Jackie Gleason, Johnny Unitas, and Joe Namath. In 1999, under the leadership of new owner Wayne Huizenga, Grande Oaks was born.

Released in 1980, *Caddyshack* is a comedy that follows caddie Danny Noonan as he works to earn money for college. The movie was green-lighted due to the overwhelming success of *Animal House*. Screenwriters Ramis, Kenney, and Doyle-Murray created a somewhat autobiographical account of their experiences in golfing. They then began the task of securing a lead to attach to the movie and ensure its future, and they recruited Rodney Dangerfield and Chevy Chase. Bill Murray was not originally a part of the cast but agreed when he was offered the opportunity to fly down for filming. His rental vehicle was a money-green Lincoln, which proved to become a memorable and nostalgic tidbit for the actor, who reminisced about it years later. After filming, he abandoned the car under a tree, where it was later found covered in debris and bird nests. Murray filmed for a total of six days, improvising the majority of his screen time.

Today, Boca Resort is a luxury Waldorf Astoria Resort and private club. The 1926 Mediterranean-inspired property spans 337 acres and offers over 1,000 guest rooms and suites among its three hotels. While the movie's golf scenes weren't shot on property, there are two 18-hole courses, as well as tennis courts, a spa, marina, watersports and a dozen dining outlets. Guests are also welcome to enjoy the Boca Beach Club, which features multiple swimming pools overlooking the Atlantic Ocean.

Address 501 E Camino Real, Boca Raton, FL 33432, +1 (561) 447-3000, www.bocaresort.com | **Getting there** From I-95: Take exit 44 and drive east on W Palmetto Park Road. Turn right on 12 Avenue, left on West Camino Real, then left to stay on West Camino Real. Resort is on the right. | **Hours** Open daily | **Tip** Enjoy 9 holes at the nearby Red Reef public golf course along the water (1221 N Ocean Boulevard, Boca Raton, www.myboca.us).

98 The Colony Hotel Haunting

Where some guests never check out

Atlantic Avenue serves as the main thoroughfare of historic downtown Delray Beach, featuring al fresco dining, galleries, shopping, and nightlife while running east to the ocean for beach access. A focal point of "The Ave" is the Colony Hotel. Built in 1926, the bright yellow and red historical landmark has a Mediterranean influence with Old Florida design. The hotel is full of character, from its lack of a bar because it was built during Prohibition, to its original manually operated elevator and telephone switchboard. It is also full of characters that are no longer with us.

For generations, the Colony Hotel has been known for its paranormal activity. Guests have reported inexplicable shadows, sounds, and pulsing lights from the first and second floors in particular. Alleged hauntings include a former staff member, who was reportedly murdered by a guest who refused to pay his hotel bill. The hotel has hosted many living celebrities and royalty alike, and there have been sightings of long and dearly departed guests, including Winston Churchill and the echoes of a singing Judy Garland, while a ghostly Duke and Duchess of Windsor have been seen shopping together, as they did in life. The hotel regularly closed for the summers, but its most loyal guests never seemed to check out. They preferred to stay and roam through the halls and common area. Much of the Martin Luther Hampton design is still intact and has been maintained, including the terrazzo floor and the roof's twin domes, preserving the locales of many a famous tale.

While the Colony Hotel is full of history, it has also developed along with its surrounding beach town. The property has adopted eco-friendly practices and continues to evolve to stay in tune with its guests' needs, while retaining its original charm. The lobby pops with vibrantly colored walls and crisp, white, wicker furnishings.

Address 525 E Atlantic Avenue, Delray Beach, FL 33483, +1 (561) 276-4123, www.colonyflorida.com | Getting there From I-95: Take exit 52 and drive east on Atlantic Avenue. Turn left onto W Atlantic Avenue. Location and parking are on the left. | Hours Daily | Tip Tour the Delray Beach area by water on a Delray Yacht Cruise (801 E Atlantic Avenue, Delray Beach, www.delraybeachcruises.com).

99 — Cornell Art Museum

From abandoned to vibrant at Old School Square

Old School Square is home to historic buildings that have taken on new purpose and life. Originally public schools, structures that were once abandoned in the 1980s were resurrected in the 1990s as a museum and performing arts venue. The Crest Theater, previously the high school, presents professional performances ranging from musical theatre and family shows to comedy and cabarets. In 2002, The Pavilion was erected, creating an outdoor venue for concerts, events, and festivals, including the annual Christmas Tree lighting.

The Cornell Art Museum here features multiple galleries with rotating exhibitions from all over the world. The museum is named in honor of George and Harriet Cornell, philanthropists who left a legacy through various contributions during their lifetime. George's familial relationships to New York's Cornell University led to their $10 million donation in funds for scholarships, the school's largest. Mr. Cornell was also the largest benefactor of his alma mater, Rollins College.

The couple championed the Square's renovation project, and they became the first private contributors. They supported the community through their contributions to local parks, hospitals, zoos, dog parks, and even a namesake café at Morikami Museum. Harriet passed away in 1999, followed by George in 2003, just weeks after his 93rd birthday.

Cornell Art Museum breathes life into the 1913 two-story schoolhouse with crisp white walls, pine hardwood floors, and windows throughout. The rooms transform with each exhibition from immersive installations and photography prints to bedazzled sculptures and mannequins draped in couture fashion. The Spotlight Gallery displays month-long collaborative exhibits highlighting local groups and organizations. During the semi-annual "Art on the Square" visitors explore the grounds outside with an al fresco fine art show.

Address 51 N Swinton Avenue, Delray Beach, FL 33444, +1 (561) 243-7922, www.cornellartmuseum.org, museuminfo@oldschool.org | Getting there From I-95: Take exit 52 and drive east on Atlantic Avenue. Turn left on N Swinton Avenue. Museum and parking on the right. | Hours Tue–Sat 10am–5pm | Tip Visit the Delray Beach Green Market at the square every Saturday from 9am–2pm during season, October through May (www.delraycra.org).

100 The Funky Biscuit

Walls of Fame at the Biscuit

The Funky Biscuit opened with the goal of being a sleepy joint, hosting local bands and serving simple Southern cuisine. However, the music world had other plans, as soon the owners found themselves booking national touring artists and hosting Rock and Roll Hall of Fame performers. Legends like Gregg Allman and David Bromberg took the stage, while a photographer friend, J. Skolnick, began to snap portraits the artists would sign on return visits. Today, it is an honor to be featured on the walls of The Funky Biscuit.

Almost called "The Forking Musicians," Biscuit's owner Al Poliak polled friends on over 100 name ideas. But after a quick search landed him on the urban definition of a funky biscuit, "a beat or a base line that rocks the membranes of your brain, brings about a feeling of hedonism and ecstasy and puts a smile on your face," the name stuck and also became a section on the menu alongside musically inspired entrees, sides, and beverages.

The Funky Biscuit restaurant and concert venue features genres from rock and roll and rhythm and blues to jazz and funk, and it has a sweet spot for New Orleans blues. Their profile gained recognition internationally through the blues community as concert-goers flew from Europe and South America to see their idols, like the late Leon Russell, play live. The energy of shows by musicians like Anders Osborne, Chris O'Leary Band, Annika Chambers, Shemekia Copeland, and Popa Chubby are memorialized in the frame photos surrounding the stage and dining room.

The Funky Biscuit runs a calendar of musical acts and performances year round. Acts like Bob Margolin who toured with Muddy Waters in the 1970s draw crowds of longtime fans. Guests enjoy po' boys and burgers with their "Rocket Man" and "Uptown Girl" specialty cocktails. Take in the sounds and revisit musical history on the walls.

Address 303 SE Mizner Boulevard, Boca Raton, FL 33432, +1 (561) 395-2929, www.funkybiscuit.com | **Getting there** From I-95: Take exit 44 and drive east on W Palmetto Park Road. Turn right on SE Mizner Boulevard. Venue will be on your right. Parking available. | **Hours** Mon–Fri 11am–3pm & 5pm–2am, Sat & Sun 5pm–2am | **Tip** Not to be confused with The Funky Biscuit, head to Funky Buddha Brewery for a locally brewed craft beer at their taproom (1201 NE 38th Street, Oakland Park, www.funkybuddhabrewery.com).

101 Joel M. Starkey Library

Pride and publications at Compass Community Center

Born of the HIV and AIDS epidemic in the 1980s, Compass Community Center became a haven for those affected by the disease. Over the decades, it has grown to become the largest gay and lesbian community center in the Southeast US, setting a high bar for centers across the country. The center has developed in its programming and expanded its focus over 30 years to become an empowering resource for the LGBTQ+ community providing educational resources, support groups, outreach, health services, youth and senior programs, events, and a Pride Business Alliance.

Joel Starkey was a pioneer for the gay community in South Florida. An activist and voice for the homosexual population, he published the *Southern Gay Liberator*, founded the Southern Gay Archives, and spearheaded various publications and organizations to unite and inform. Starkey worked to create safe spaces where young adults could congregate, feel accepted, and flourish, like the Gay Academic Union at Florida International University. Starkey died in 1992 at the young age of 45, after his own battle with HIV and AIDS.

His legacy lives on in those he inspired to continue his efforts, and also in his namesake library at Compass, which includes a collection of over 1,500 LGBTQ+ titles. The library offers works by LGBTQ+ authors, history books, books on how to speak with children about HIV and AIDS or what family means, plus many works of fiction, reference books, and much more. You can even peruse the collection online to pick out some books before you get there.

The center's efforts have strived to engage, empower, and enrich the lives of lesbian, gay, bisexual, transgender, and queer (LGBTQ+) people and those impacted by HIV and AIDS. The center participates in the annual Lake Worth Street Painting Festival, the nation-wide Dining Out For Life program, and the Palm Beach Pride events.

Address 201 N Dixie Highway, Lake Worth, FL 33460, +1 (561) 533-9699, www.compassglcc.com | Getting there From I-95: Take exit 64 and drive east on 10th Avenue N. Turn right on US Highway 1. Turn right on 2nd Avenue North. Center located on the right. | Hours Mon–Thu 10am–7pm, Fri 10am–5pm | Tip Enjoy a cocktail and game of billiards at the neighborhood gay bar, Mad Hatter Lounge (1532 N Dixie Highway, Lake Worth).

102 Marty's Cube at Boca Muse
Push to start

Boca Museum, or "Boca Muse," is considered one of South Florida's premier cultural institutions, featuring permanent and traveling exhibits and collections. Before you even enter the door, the immersive experience begins with *Marty's Cube*, a sculpture guests are welcome to spin on its base as they pass. The 1983 piece by Tony Rosenthal is composed of painted steel measuring 175 inches on each side and is similar to *The Cube* in New York City that inspired many Halloween costumes and was met with great celebration on its 2016 return. The cube is unlike the majority of exhibits that grace the museum, as visitors are invited to touch and interact with the monumental structure.

Born Bernard Rosenthal in Highland Park, Illinois in 1914, "Tony" received his first public art commission for the 1939 World's Fair in Queens, NY, where he installed *The Nubian Slave*. In the 1960s, he moved away from figurative sculpture and into abstract geometric at the urging of his art dealer Sam Kootz, of Picasso fame. Over the course of his career, his collections ranged from cubes to stick figures to discs, often hiding symbolism and a deeper meaning. Rosenthal passed away on July 28, 2009 in Southampton, New York.

This particular cube, one of a handful created by Rosenthal, was named after Marty Margulies. Margulies was a real estate developer, art collector, and enthusiast based out of Miami. He amassed a large collection of art, valued at an estimated $800 million, which was displayed for free publicly on Grove Isle before being distributed to various places due to issues with the island management. *Marty's Cube* called the Florida International University home for over a decade, where students began a tradition of spinning the cube for good luck on exams. After it was removed, students created an online cube.

Address 501 Plaza Real, Boca Raton, FL 33432, +1 (561) 392-2500, www.bocamuseum.org |
Getting there From I-95: Take exit 48 and drive east on Spanish River Boulevard. Turn right
on N Dixie Highway. Turn left on NE 8th Street, then right on N Federal Highway, and left
on NW 5th Street. Museum on the left. Street parking and parking garage available. | Hours
Tue, Wed & Fri 10am–5pm, Thu 10am–8pm, Sat & Sun noon–5pm | Tip Plan for a day
at Mizner Park and enjoy the dining, retail, and entertainment offerings including a movie
theater (327 Plaza Real, Boca Raton, www.miznerpark.com).

103 Nomad Surf Shop

Over 50 years of stoke

Opened in 1968, Nomad Surf Shop is a family owned and operated staple for locals and visitors who are in the market for surfboards, beach clothing, and gear. Steeped in local history, this casual surf shop has catered to generations of ocean lovers, being the oldest of its kind in South Florida. The faded orange building with its bright blue awning is a local icon. Over the years, the property has expanded, and the uses of each space have changed as they have been absorbed into the business.

Nomad began with the late Ron Heavyside. He realized his passion for building surfboards in his teens while he was still in school. Along with a handful of friends, Heavyside rented an industrial space to build boards. The name "Nomad" came from the idea of surfers who wander the world looking for the perfect wave. While his father ran a television repair business, Heavyside took up a small portion of the showroom to display his custom surfboards and sell apparel. Later with his wife Beth, he expanded his enterprise with the purchase of the bar next door and then the gas station. Nomad Surfboards became Nomad Surf Shop, offering an array of clothing, equipment, and accessories.

The business has seen the ebbs and flows of the Heavyside family through the breakup and later the passing of both Beth and Ron. Today, their sons, Ryan and Ronnie, run the shop and have brought it back to its former glory.

Shoppers are greeted with a sense of nostalgia, as the old school vibe of the shop has been maintained and nurtured. Racks of apparel feature Nomad designs, like their anniversary "50 Years of Stoke" graphic tee, branded sweaters, and "Love Surf Nomad" ponchos. Whether you are looking to purchase a new bikini or simply take in the decaled walls of this legendary boutique, make sure to visit their food truck in the parking lot for a cold brew coffee or açaí bowl.

Address 4655 N Ocean Boulevard, Boynton Beach, FL 33435, +1 (561) 272-2882, www.nomadsurf1968.com | Getting there From I-95: Take exit 56 and drive east on Woolbright Road. Cross the bridge and turn right on N Ocean Boulevard. Store and parking on the left. | Hours Mon – Sat 10am – 6:30pm, Sun 10am – 6pm | Tip Book a surf lesson at the nearby Waves Surf Academy (1875 S Ocean Boulevard, Delray Beach, www.wavessurfacademy.com).

104 — Omote-Senke Tea Ceremony

Tradition and culture whisked together

A center for Japanese art, culture, and botanicals, the Morikami Museum and Japanese Gardens location just west of Delray Beach has an interesting backstory. In the early 20th century Jo Sakai, a Miyazu native, returned home to Japan to gather farmers for a collaborative effort in northern Boca Raton. Their colony, Yamato, didn't yield the intended results, leading to the disbursement of the group. But they created a lasting link between the Japanese and American cultures.

Honoring Japanese history and traditions, Morikami opened in 1977. A permanent exhibit shows in the original museum building, the Yamato-kan, displaying the history of the farm colony alongside an interactive, contemporary exploration of Japanese culture. Inspired by traditional Japanese design, the building reflects a villa with an open-air courtyard at its center. A larger museum was built to accommodate more visitors in the 1990s with galleries, a theater, library, classrooms, café, and an authentic tea house. In 2001, the property revealed newly expanded and renovated 16-acre gardens within the 200-acre park. You can explore nature trails, visit the bonsai collection, and observe koi fish, while experiencing the story-telling Hoichi Kurisu design.

A highlight of the museum, the Seishin-an Tea House welcomes guests to experience *Omote-Senke*-style tea ceremonies on select Saturdays and also offers tea ceremony classes and workshops. Of the over 7,000 artifacts on-site, 500 pieces make up the tea ceremony collection. One of three *san-senke* schools, the Omote-Senke school was founded by tea master Sen no Rikyū and is distinguished by its tea whisking and foam style. The "grass hut"-style structure is unpretentious and creates an atmosphere of tranquility and respect. The ceremonies involve strict etiquette but produce a visually appealing, graceful experience that pleases the senses.

Address 4000 Morikami Park Road, Delray Beach, FL 33446, +1 (561) 495-0233, www.morikami.org | Getting there From I-95: Take exit 51 and drive west on Linton Boulevard. Turn left on Jog Road. Turn right on Morikami Road. Turn left on Puzzle Place. Turn right on Morikami Park Road. Museum on left and parking lot on right. | Hours Tue–Sun 10am–5pm | Tip Learn more about the history of the Yamato Colony and area at the Boca Raton Historical Society and Museum (71 N Federal Highway, Boca Raton, www.bocahistory.org).

105— Polo Hall of Fame

Portraits of horses to remember

The game of polo dates back thousands of years. Though its exact origins are lost to its long history, the game as it is now played is believed to have started in India. The first formal polo club was founded in the mid-1800s by British tea farmers visiting Silchar, now considered the birthplace of modern polo, also known as "The Sport of Kings." The Museum of Polo at Lake Worth houses a collection of documents and artifacts relating to the sport and history of polo. The Hall of Fame honors the icons of the game that descends on the village of Wellington each year.

Melinda Brewer is an award-winning fine arts wildlife painter, who has found a niche in the appreciation and commemoration of horses. Offering to produce portraits of Hall of Fame ponies, her ensuing collection became a highlight of their exhibit, "Horses to Remember." The watercolor depictions pay homage to the inductees and their contribution to the sport. This collection of equine portraits includes ponies like Chica Boom, a 1982 and 1984 Hartman Trophy winner owned by Hall of Famer Bart Evans. Ideal polo horses are not only measured by their physical attributes, but also their temperament and training. Players typically ride multiple ponies per match to allow for rest during the two hours of play.

Since 2000, over 40 portraits have been painted and displayed at the Polo Museum. The compilation is a tribute to some of the greatest ponies to play the game and an acknowledgement of the importance of the equine teammates that the human players ride during gameplay.

With a collection of important artwork, mallets, and saddles, as well as trophies, records, and print publications, The Museum of Polo encapsulates and celebrates the sport of polo and provides a deeper look into its history. Every February, players and ponies are recognized during the Hall of Fame Induction Awards Dinner Gala.

Address 9011 Lake Worth Road, Lake Worth, FL 33467, +1 (561) 969-3210, www.polomuseum.com | Getting there From I-95: Take exit 66 and drive west on Forest Hill Boulevard. Turn left onto Pinehurst Drive, then right onto FL-802 West. Turn right and parking, and the destination is on the left. | Hours See website for seasonal hours | Tip Catch a match at the International Polo Club in Wellington (3667 120th Avenue S, Wellington, www.ipc.coth.com).

106 Saltwater Brewery

Explore the depths of beer inspired by the sea

A team of lifelong friends and family converged at Delray Beach's once desolate large red barn to create a dream business. Previously a seed-and-feed farm supply store turned antique market, the founders of Saltwater Brewery breathed life back into the wood structure in 2013. This 1950s building, that might have seen demolition given owners other than the Gove family, was re-imagined with its own pine beams and doors incorporated back into the interior design. Original elements can be seen in the floors, ceilings, tabletops and bar.

Approaching the barn, visitors are greeted with a beer garden of tables and cornhole boards, usually surrounded by craft beer lovers. Once inside the Reef Tasting Room the true size of the structure becomes apparent with multiple seating areas, a long bar born of the barn's past and a glass wall allowing patrons to gaze into the brewing room of towering steel tanks. The brewery houses a state-of-the-art canning and labeling system that enables Saltwater to make and distribute special releases, along with their three core beers: Screamin' Reels IPA, Sea Cow Milk Stout, and LocAle Golden Ale. Visitors are welcome to enjoy their beverages on-site or take home a growler of the rotating chalkboard of offerings.

Inspired by their love of the ocean, the brewers use a "depth chart" to depict their beer styles by color and alcohol content. Co-owner Peter Agardy painted a mural of the chart in the brewery that is used to name the beers and for guests to use when selecting a pint. Guests can enjoy their Coastal, Reef, and Offshore series, ranging from 3.5% ABV to upwards of 11%. All of their beer names and insignias pay homage to the ocean. The owners' concern for the world's waters led to their involvement in the design of an ocean-friendly six-pack ring system that is biodegradable, edible, and safer for marine life.

Address 1701 W Atlantic Avenue, Delray Beach, FL 33444, +1 (561) 865-5373, www.saltwaterbrewery.com | Getting there From I-95: Take exit 52 and drive west on Atlantic Avenue for 0.25 mile. Make a right on NW 18th Avenue. Brewery is on right. Parking in front. | Hours Sun–Wed noon–11pm, Thu–Sat noon–midnight | Tip Cruise the craft brewery "Ale Trail" of the Palm Beaches on a group or private tour by the Damn Good Beer Bus (www.damngoodbeerbus.com).

107 Sandoway Discovery Center

Dip your toes in the sands of time

In the mid-1990s, after decades as a private residence, the J. B. Evans House was purchased and restored to become what is now Sandoway Discovery Center. The center offers excursions, classes, and exhibits about Florida's natural environment. Feed stingrays or join a beach cleanup at this beachfront location that offers easy access to oceanic marine life, coral, seashells, and plants. The coastal ecosystems and marine life center is working to create the next generation of environmental scientists and conservationists.

You must experience the house too. J. B. Evans was a businessman from the North, who made his money in agricultural endeavors, brokering produce out of Deerfield Beach. Built for his retirement, his historic 1936 resort colonial-style home is characteristic of its era and reminiscent of the upper classes during the Great Depression.

The work of architect Samuel Ogren Sr., Evans' two-story frame house was designed to reflect the times with hints of modesty, featuring white clapboard siding, green wooden shutters, pine flooring, and cypress ceilings. Ogren was the area's first resident architect, and he is credited with over 200 private and public buildings in the county. Born in China to Swedish missionaries, the family fled during the Boxer Rebellion. His father lost his life during their escape, and his mother made it to the United States with their two children.

Eventually, Ogren settled in Delray Beach, where his breezy resort style became the signature look of this small town in its homes and schools. In 2002, the J. B. Evans House was added to the National Register of Historic Places, protecting one of the few of its kind along the Delray Beach waterfront. The Sandoway Discovery Center is a fitting tribute to the architect who found success and created the signature style of his adopted hometown.

Address 142 S Ocean Boulevard, Delray Beach, FL 33483, +1 (561) 274-7263, www.sandoway.org | Getting there From I-95: Take exit 56 and drive east on Woolbright Road. Turn right onto Florida A1A S / N Ocean Boulevard. Parking and center will be on the right. | Hours Tue–Sat 10am–4pm, Sun noon–4pm | Tip Visit the Old School Square Gymnasium, now known as The Fieldhouse, to see another Ogren design (51 N Swinton Avenue, Delray Beach, www.oldschoolsquare.org).

108 Silverball Museum

Play the classics

Easy to spot with its wild, vibrantly muraled walls, Silverball Museum is just as animated on the inside. Rows of vintage pinball and arcade games create aisles of dancing lights and theme song sounds. Featuring over 150 games, including iterations of PacMan, antique pinball games like Centigrade 73, and lines of Skeeball, the collection is both entertaining and nostalgic. The best part is here visitors get to play the exhibits.

The name "Silverball" is a nod to the play piece of a pinball machine. Players use a plunger to release a metallic ball into a tilted game board that has seen many changes throughout the years. While the components of a pinball machine may seem instinctive today, each mechanism was introduced by designers over the years. Original machines were manually bumped and tilted by the player. In fact, the game was so random that for decades it was illegal. Authorities felt the lack of skill involved constituted a form of gambling. Police performed raids, where machines were destroyed like whisky during Prohibition. The pinball machine became a speakeasy item and later a symbol for rebellious pop culture characters, like Fonzie in *Happy Days*. Over time, bumpers and eventually the flipper created an argument for the ban to be revisited. In 1976, the task was left to Roger Sharpe to prove his skill could win a game of pinball. After his original machine was replaced by a backup game, a lucky shot call overturned the ban.

Silverball Museum games are set to "free play" so you don't need to bring your own quarters. You can pay by the hour or purchase membership levels for unlimited monthly play. The collection features games by pinball giants Gottlieb, Bally's, Midway, Stern, and Williams. The upstairs balcony includes a restaurant for casual dining, private parties, or to enjoy an adult beverage and watch the gamers below.

Address 19 NE 3rd Avenue, Delray Beach, FL 33483, +1 (561) 266-3294, www.silverballmuseum.com | Getting there From I-95: Take exit 52 and drive east on Atlantic Avenue. Turn left on NW 1st Avenue. Turn right on NW 1st Street. Turn right on NE 3rd Avenue. Museum is on the left. | Hours Sun–Thu noon–10pm, Fri & Sat noon–midnight | Tip Explore Museum 66, an industrial venue with rare muscle cars, vintage pinball machines, and a private event space (2051 High Ridge Road, Boynton Beach, www.museum66.com).

109__ Spady Museum
Take a ride and remember

Take a ride through the five historic districts of Delray Beach on the Ride & Remember Tour. An offering of The Spady Cultural Heritage Museum, this interactive experience allows guests to step into each district while learning about its heritage, significance and development. The Spady Museum, located in the former home of the late Solomon D. Spady, is the only Black history museum and cultural center of its kind in Palm Beach County. Embracing and celebrating the history of Americans of African, Caribbean, and Haitian descent, the museum serves as an epicenter of cultural history, artifacts, ideas, and community.

Solomon D. Spady was born in 1887 in Virginia, where he became a scientist and teacher. In 1922, Spady relocated to Delray Beach becoming just the third African American principal and teacher in the area at the now-named George Washington Carver High School. In 1926, he and his wife Jessie constructed their Mission Revival-style home on Blackmer Street, the first in the area to have indoor plumbing, a telephone and electricity. Enrollment at the school multiplied under Spady's guidance while class offerings and extracurricular activities expanded. His impact on his students and the entire community over his three decades of service was recognized with the naming of S. D. Spady Elementary School. Both he and his wife are credited with being some of the strongest voices for the African American community in Delray Beach's history. In 1999, his family accepted the Unsung Hero award on his behalf for *Great Floridians 2000*.

Today, the Spady house serves as the museum, with its white stucco exterior, copper trim, and hardwood floors. The museum features exhibits within the gallery space, provides house tours, hosts a series of events, provides educational programs for children, and serves as a place for "expanding and preserving our cultural heritage."

Address 170 NW 5th Avenue, Delray Beach, FL 33444, +1 (561) 279-8883, www.spadymuseum.com | Getting there From I-95: Take exit 52 and drive east on Atlantic Avenue. Turn left on NW 5th Avenue. Museum and parking on left. | Hours Tue–Sat 11am–4pm | Tip Visit the nearby St. Olive Baptist Church where Spady was heavily involved as a church clerk, group leader and Sunday School teacher (40 NW 4th Avenue, Delray Beach, FL 33444, www.greatermountolivembc.org).

110_ Taru Garden
Lush oasis in the heart of downtown

Sundy House is an award-winning restaurant, boutique inn, and event space. A restored 1902 Queen Anne Victorian home with a wrapping veranda, it is the oldest home in Delray Beach. Windowed doors pull back to reveal the outdoors in the Fresco Room, while twinkling lighting and greenery dangle from Dade pine ceiling beams to create a seamless transition to the surrounding gardens. Particularly popular for brunch and weddings, the venue is also home to Taru Garden.

Once the site of a dilapidated apartment building and notoriously drug-friendly parking lot, it took the vision of Tom Worrell, along with the help of Rickard Wilson – and over a million dollars – to reimagine, plant, and bring the garden to life. In a lush acre featuring over 5,000 plants and varieties of foliage, guests will discover tropical fruit trees, bamboo groves, fish ponds, and waterfalls as they make their way through this enchanting space. Over 100 of the plants yield edible fruits, flowers, or herbs used in the kitchen. Within the garden is the naturalized Cenote Pond, designed to resemble the stunning *cenotes* of the Yucatan, with black marcite, limestone boulders, tropical surroundings, and freshwater marine life.

While the garden is a utopia of greenery, the house restaurant itself is a piece of local history. Originally built as Mayor John Sundy's six-bedroom family home, it centered as the city's first church, bank, and schoolhouse. Sundy came to the area as a superintendent from Florida East Coast Railway, working for Henry Flagler (see ch. 73). He settled in the area when the railroad continued south, and he became one of the early pioneers of what was Linton at the time. Sundy opened a feed and fertilizer business, while his wife Elizabeth taught children in their home and immersed herself in the community. Today, the Sundy House welcomes guests and diners.

Address 106 S Swinton Avenue, Delray Beach, FL 33444, +1 (877) 439-9601, www.sundyhouse.com, info@sundyhouse.com | **Getting there** From I-95: Take exit 52 and drive east on Atlantic Avenue. Turn right on South Swinton Avenue. House and parking on right. | **Hours** See website for dining hours | **Tip** Walk the tree-lined paths and visit the grave of John Sundy at the Delray Beach Memorial Gardens (700 SW 8th Avenue, Delray Beach).

111 Wick Costume Museum

Costumes straight from Broadway's stages

Some of the most iconic Broadway costumes to ever grace the stage can be found within the Costume Museum at the Wick Theatre. Featuring wardrobes from over 85 Broadway productions, the collection has been passionately curated by founder and executive producer Marilynn A. Wick over the course of four decades. Estimated to be worth over $22 million, the collection has been featured nationally on *The Today Show*, in *People* magazine, and on the pages of *Vogue*.

The Costume Museum gives theater lovers a chance to explore their favorite shows' attire up close and personal with rotating exhibits of costumes and props, and fans come back regularly. Collections have included "Bling," which was a collaboration with the Liberace Foundation for the Performing and Creative Arts, and "The Roaring 20s," which featured costumes from Broadway shows set in the 1920s, including *Thoroughly Modern Millie, The Drowsy Chaperone*, along with sections honoring the Suffragists and famed designer Erte. Guests are invited to take a package tour, which may include lunch, a cabaret performance, or a matinee show. Lunch is served at The Tavern at Wick, a unique dining experience that pays homage to New York City's Tavern on the Green, complete with the crystal and amber chandelier that previously hung in the original tavern's foyer.

Wick grew a handful of Santa Claus costumes into one of the largest costume rental companies and theatrical distributors in the country. Her collection has been used by clients including Ringling Brothers Circus and has outfitted theatres across the nation. Wick transformed the previous Caldwell Theatre Company space into what is now the theater and museum, a regional venue that has been well respected throughout the industry since 2013. Theater lovers can enjoy musicals and cabarets among the calendar of productions.

Address 7901 N Federal Highway, Boca Raton, FL 33487, +1 (561) 995-2333,
www.thewick.org | Getting there From I-95: Take exit 51 and drive east on Linton
Boulevard. Turn right on US Highway 1. Museum is on the right. | Hours See website for
hours and special events | Tip Lake Worth Playhouse is said to be the haunting grounds
of Lucien Oakley, one of the brothers who built the theater in 1924 (713 Lake Avenue,
Lake Worth, www.lakeworthplayhouse.org).

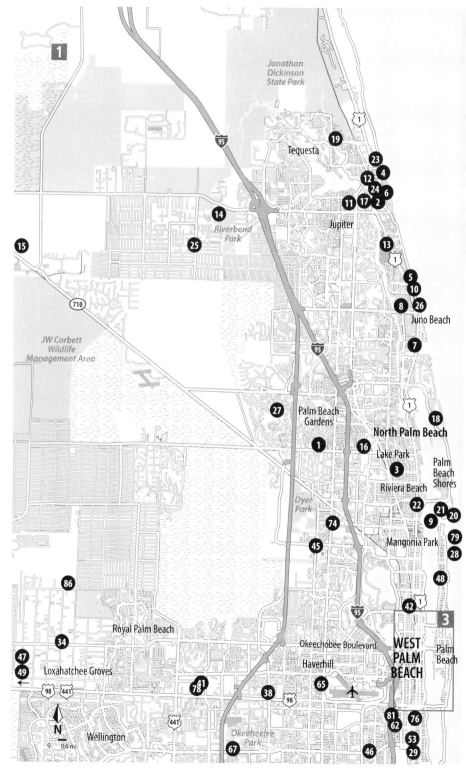

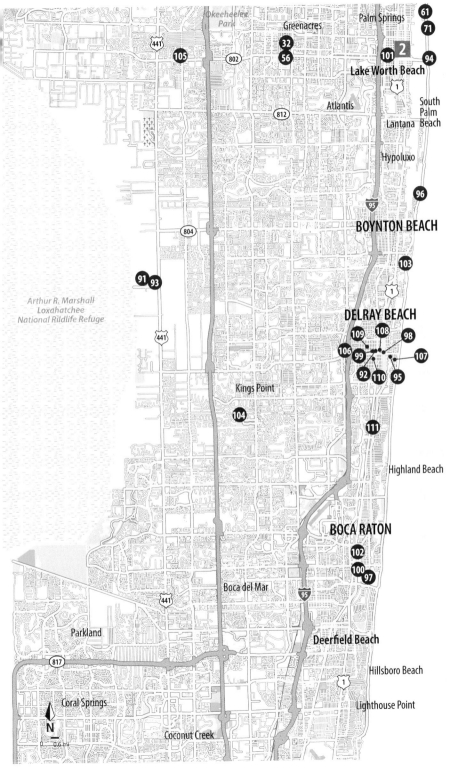

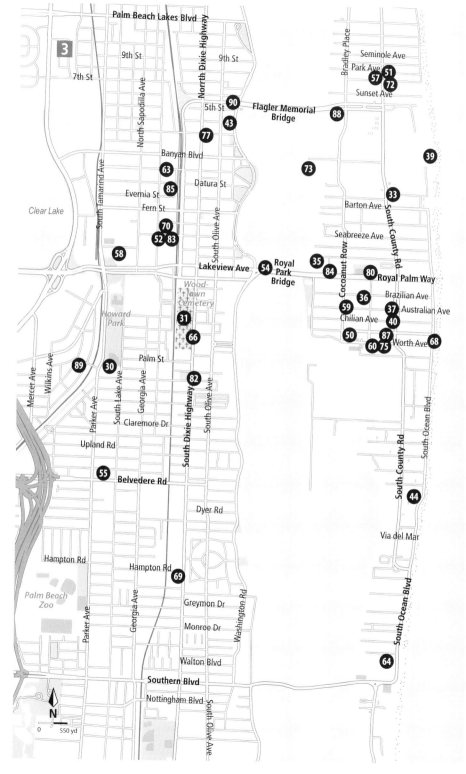

Gordon Streisand
**111 Places in Miami and the
Keys That You Must Not Miss**
ISBN 978-3-95451-644-5

Travis Swann Taylor
**111 Places in Atlanta
That You Must Not Miss**
ISBN 978-3-7408-0747-4

Dana DuTerroil, Joni Fincham,
Daniel Jackson
**111 Places in Houston
That You Must Not Miss**
ISBN 978-3-7408-0896-9

Kelsey Roslin, Nick Yeager,
Jesse Pitzler
**111 Places in Austin
That You Must Not Miss**
ISBN 978-3-7408-0748-1

Katrina Nattress, Jason Quigley
**111 Places in Portland
That You Must Not Miss**
ISBN 978-3-7408-0750-4

Floriana Petersen, Steve Werney
**111 Places in Silicon Valley
That You Must Not Miss**
ISBN 978-3-7408-0493-0

Floriana Petersen, Steve Werney
**111 Places in San Francisco
That You Must Not Miss**
ISBN 978-3-95451-609-4

Amy Bizzarri, Susie Inverso
**111 Places in Chicago
That You Must Not Miss**
ISBN 978-3-7408-0156-4

Michelle Madden, Janet McMillan
**111 Places in Milwaukee
That You Must Not Miss**
ISBN 978-3-7408-0491-6

Elisabeth Larsen
111 Places in the Twin Cities
That You Must Not Miss
ISBN 978-3-7408-0029-1

Sandra Gurvis, Mitch Geiser
111 Places in Columbus
That You Must Not Miss
ISBN 978-3-7408-0600-2

Jo-Anne Elikann
111 Places in New York
That You Must Not Miss
ISBN 978-3-95451-052-8

Wendy Lubovich, Jean Hodgens
111 Places in the Hamptons
That You Must Not Miss
ISBN 978-3-7408-0751-1

Wendy Lubovich, Ed Lefkowicz
111 Museums in New York
That You Must Not Miss
ISBN 978-3-7408-0379-7

Leslie Adatto, Clay Williams
111 Rooftops in New York
That You Must Not Miss
ISBN 978-3-7408-0495-4

John Major, Ed Lefkowicz
111 Places in Brooklyn
That You Must Not Miss
ISBN 978-3-7408-0380-3

Kevin C. Fitzpatrick, Joe Conzo
111 Places in the Bronx
That You Must Not Miss
ISBN 978-3-7408-0492-3

Joe DiStefano, Clay Williams
111 Places in Queens
That You Must Not Miss
ISBN 978-3-7408-0020-8

Andréa Seiger, John Dean
111 Places in Washington
That You Must Not Miss
ISBN 978-3-7408-0258-5

Allison Robicelli, John Dean
111 Places in Baltimore
That You Must Not Miss
ISBN 978-3-7408-0158-8

Dave Doroghy, Graeme Menzies
111 Places in Vancouver
That You Must Not Miss
ISBN 978-3-7408-0494-7

Anita Mai Genua,
Clare Davenport,
Elizabeth Lenell Davies
111 Places in Toronto
That You Must Not Miss
ISBN 978-3-7408-0257-8

Benjamin Haas, Leonie Friedrich
111 Places in Buenos Aires
That You Must Not Miss
ISBN 978-3-7408-0260-8

Beate C. Kirchner,
Jorge Vasconcellos
111 Places in Rio de Janeiro
That You Must Not Miss
ISBN 978-3-7408-0262-2

Christoph Hein, Sabine Hein
111 Places in Singapore
That You Shouldn't Miss
ISBN 978-3-7408-0382-7

Christine Izeki, Björn Neumann
111 Places in Tokyo
That You Shouldn't Miss
ISBN 978-3-7408-0024-6

John Sykes, Birgit Weber
111 Places in London
That You Shouldn't Miss
ISBN 978-3-95451-346-8

Photo Credits

Censored at The Breakers (ch 39): Courtesy of The Breakers Palm Beach

Caddy Shack Was Here (ch. 97): Courtesy of Boca Raton Resort & Club

Art Credits

Brewhouse Gallery (ch. 3): Mural Projects by (L to R) Eduardo Mendieta, Steven Marino, and Amanda Valdes

Shopping Mall Masterpiece (ch. 23): A Tribe Called Tequesta by Jason Newsted (April 2018)

Big Dog Ranch Rescue (ch. 34): Sign by Thomas Goetz

Heau (ch. 54): Artwork by "Hula" Sean Yoro

Cornell Art Museum (ch. 99): Designs by Amanda Perna

Thank you to my wonderful parents, Carol and Woody, for being the biggest cheerleaders I could have ever asked for. My husband Andrew for always supporting my endeavors and crazy ideas – I love you. Our beautiful girls, Emilia and Audrey, for changing my whole world and making me the proudest mama. My best friend Leigh Riemer, for introducing me to this series and always picking up wherever we leave off. Thank you to my family and friends who encourage me every day and to Emons Verlag, Karen Seiger, Jakob Takos, Laura Olk, and Lucia Marin for helping make this book a reality.

Cristyle Egitto

Thank you, 111 Places, for giving me such an incredible opportunity. Working with Cristyle Egitto has been one of the greatest experiences alone. Thanks to Pumphouse Coffee for fueling my mornings and positive energy. and to all who helped guide me throughout this process. To Geo Lehn for taking the day to drive me to my locations when I had car troubles, for being a certified drone pilot to help with a shot, and for being a good friend. My music community – thank you for always supporting and sharing my content. To the most important person in my life, Tia. you're the first person I took a portrait of and have always stayed patient through my progress. I would be lost in my creative journey if it wasn't for you.

Jakob Takos

Cristyle Wood Egitto is a South Florida native, born in Miami and raised in Palm Beach County. A lover of her hometown, she has always had an affinity for the area's lifestyle, culture and history and is actively involved in the community. Cristyle resides in North County with her family and writes the food and lifestyle blog *Eat Palm Beach*.

Jakob Takos is a Palm Beach native who was born and raised in Jupiter, Florida. His love for photography has led him to start his own creative company called Nothing Negative. When he isn't behind the lens, you can find him traveling and playing guitar as a singer and songwriter. He credits his dad for teaching him the beauty of paying close attention to the details in life.